CENTRED

THE WOMEN OF THE WOMEN'S CENTRE

EDITED BY

Natalie Simpson

the
**WOMEN'S
CENTRE**

CALGARY, ALBERTA

Canadian Cataloguing in Publication Data

Main entry under title:

Centred

ISBN 0-9687641-0-X

1. Women's Centre (Calgary, Alta.) 2. Women--Alberta--Calgary-- Biography. 3. Women--Services for--Alberta--Calgary. I. Simpson, Natalie, 1975- II. Women's Centre (Calgary, Alta.)

HV1448.C32C3 2000   362.83'097123'38 C00-911019-4

The publishers thank the Calgary Community Lottery Board for the generous grant that made this publication possible.

The editor also acknowledges the support of Lucette Simpson and Lanagan Financial Services.

Printed and Bound in Canada by Artline Printing.

Cover Design and Layout: *Irena Ho*|vissiondesign.com:

cover painting: *Li - oil on board by* **Irena Ho**

The Women's Centre
644B 1ˢᵗ Avenue NE
Calgary, Alberta
T2E OB6

The writing of this book coincided with the **World March of Women**, *which took place from April to October 2000. The* **World March of Women** *is an international effort to end poverty and violence against women.*

We dedicate this book to that effort.

FOREWORD

We thank the women of the Women's Centre of Calgary who generously shared their stories with us. Their stories speak to our souls. They demonstrate fragility, strength, sadness and joy. We hope that they will speak to you and spread the sense of community we build together at the Women's Centre.

The Women's Centre of Calgary is a welcoming, accessible, and free drop-in peer program. The Centre provides peer support and opportunities for women to help women.

The Centre offers a legal advice clinic held weekly with the assistance of volunteer lawyers. Personal development groups are very popular at the Centre; they include a women's safety group and a Practice English group, where women whose first language is not English come to socialize, talk, and get facilitated help with their English skills. At collective kitchens organized in nearby community centres, women come together to cook and share the results of their labour. The Centre houses a resource room and provides free access to office equipment, a library, and a variety of workshops. Finally, emergency assistance is available as well as crisis intervention and referrals to other local agencies.

The Women's Centre encourages the growth of women's creativity, abilities and decision-making skills, and provides a safe place for women to build support networks. Financial support from the United Way of Calgary, the City of Calgary, the Calgary Community Lottery Board, Petro-Canada, and a multitude of individual and business donors makes this work possible.

JANE CAWTHORNE

CONTENTS

INTRODUCTION
Susan Gillies

There has been a Women's Centre in Calgary, in one form or another, for a long time. The Centre first opened in the early 1970s as part of the YWCA. In the years since, it has been closed a couple of times due to lack of funding. When the YWCA closed the Centre in June 1997, the community rallied to reopen it as an independent organization. It reopened in October 1997, under the umbrella of Oxfam-Canada, and in July 2000 received its own charitable status from Revenue-Canada.

Why a Women's Centre? A small number of us have never had a happy, non-violent relationship with a man, but most of us have fathers, partners, sons, or brothers who we love very much. We have male friends, neighbours, and colleagues who we like and respect. Some of those men are volunteers at the Centre. No, we do not hate men, but we do recognize a gender gap.

There is a gap in the wages men and women earn and in the amount of childcare and housework they say they do. There is a gap in the amount and kind of violence men and women face. There is a gap in the way they vote and the issues they think are important. There is a gap in the gender ratio around boardroom tables, in government, in higher levels of management—and almost anywhere agendas and policies are set.

And there are differences in our awareness of those gaps and in how they affect our lives. For women, those gaps can mean not having enough money to pay the rent or feed the kids. They can mean not feeling safe getting to your car in the parkade, or not feel-

1

ing safe in your own home. They mean not feel

not getting promoted, not being part of the

sadness, frustration, and anger about those ga

There are differences in the way men and

ences in our understanding of our selves and o

why the Women's Centre has survived. It's in

be in a place where women set the agenda, wh

extent or another, experienced the impact of

The Women's Centre has survived and

over the years. Today we have no criteria a

Centre or what problems you can bring to us

have no forms, no waiting lists, and no time re

drop in, with all your issues, for however lo

of work that would make efficiency experts c

years the Women's Centre has carried on and ev

needs—always with very few staff and many

Today the Women's Centre has about three s

unteers, and approximately 1,000 client conta

"Client" is a term we use for statistics

women—women working, women voluntee

the Centre. At any given time roles may shift

black and white at the Centre. We know all

and solutions, weaknesses and strengths. Ano

all.

Over and over, women say that they fe

Centre. Safe to seek and to give help. Safe to

to feel sad, frustrated, and angry, safe to laugh

of few days during my time at the Centre w

by a woman's story. I can't remember a day

am always in awe of women's commitment

Commitment like that of Jill's and Lind

volunteering at the Women's Centre for 18

INTRODUCTION
Susan Gillies

There has been a Women's Centre in Calgary, in one form or another, for a long time. The Centre first opened in the early 1970s as part of the YWCA. In the years since, it has been closed a couple of times due to lack of funding. When the YWCA closed the Centre in June 1997, the community rallied to reopen it as an independent organization. It reopened in October 1997, under the umbrella of Oxfam-Canada, and in July 2000 received its own charitable status from Revenue-Canada.

Why a Women's Centre? A small number of us have never had a happy, non-violent relationship with a man, but most of us have fathers, partners, sons, or brothers who we love very much. We have male friends, neighbours, and colleagues who we like and respect. Some of those men are volunteers at the Centre. No, we do not hate men, but we do recognize a gender gap.

There is a gap in the wages men and women earn and in the amount of childcare and housework they say they do. There is a gap in the amount and kind of violence men and women face. There is a gap in the way they vote and the issues they think are important. There is a gap in the gender ratio around boardroom tables, in government, in higher levels of management—and almost anywhere agendas and policies are set.

And there are differences in our awareness of those gaps and in how they affect our lives. For women, those gaps can mean not having enough money to pay the rent or feed the kids. They can mean not feeling safe getting to your car in the parkade, or not feel-

1

ing safe in your own home. They mean not feeling that you are heard, not getting promoted, not being part of the system. Women feel sadness, frustration, and anger about those gaps.

There are differences in the way men and women work, differences in our understanding of our selves and our world. I think that's why the Women's Centre has survived. It's important sometimes to be in a place where women set the agenda, where we have all, to one extent or another, experienced the impact of those gaps.

The Women's Centre has survived and thrived in its own way over the years. Today we have no criteria about who can use the Centre or what problems you can bring to us. For the most part, we have no forms, no waiting lists, and no time restrictions. You can just drop in, with all your issues, for however long you need. It's a way of work that would make efficiency experts crazy. But for almost 30 years the Women's Centre has carried on and evolved to meet women's needs—always with very few staff and many volunteers and clients. Today the Women's Centre has about three staff positions, 230 volunteers, and approximately 1,000 client contacts a month.

"Client" is a term we use for statistics. At the Centre we're all women—women working, women volunteering, and women using the Centre. At any given time roles may shift, for there is very little black and white at the Centre. We know all women have problems and solutions, weaknesses and strengths. And we try to share them all.

Over and over, women say that they feel safe in the Women's Centre. Safe to seek and to give help. Safe to express themselves, safe to feel sad, frustrated, and angry, safe to laugh and rejoice. I can think of few days during my time at the Centre when I wasn't saddened by a woman's story. I can't remember a day without laughter. And I am always in awe of women's commitment and strength.

Commitment like that of Jill's and Linda's. They have each been volunteering at the Women's Centre for 18 years. They have sat on boards and committees; raised funds; taken part in numerous planning sessions, studies and evaluations; and fought to keep the Centre alive. They have each volunteered once a week on the resource desk, answering phones and doing peer support. And they have done it with grace and humour for 18 years.

And the commitment of our many volunteers. We had to staff two fund-raisers—a football game and two days of casino—in one week this summer; there were 72 long shifts to cover. Enough women were there, along with their families and friends, that no one had to do double duty.

I'm in awe of the strength of women like Brenda, Rose, and Mary. When Brenda came to the Centre she was new to the city. She was living in uneasy shared accommodation and was job hunting. Brenda came to the Centre nearly every day, for hours each day, to fax resumes and phone employers. It took nearly a year, but she never gave up. When she finally found a job it only lasted two weeks. But Brenda just started again. Today she is working and living in happier circumstances. Between work shifts she comes to the Centre and helps with what she can.

Rose, who has a chronic illness, left an abusive relationship and raised her children while living in poverty. She was evicted time after time; the rent wasn't paid because her child support wasn't paid. There was never enough money for clothes and food, let alone for the medications she needed. She scrambled to find help to get her kids swimming lessons and school supplies. For years, as she fought pain and exhaustion, she also fought and pleaded with a system that never provided enough to make ends meet, that never offered the kind of support she needed. Her kids are on their own now, so in middle age, still living in poverty and coping with a debilitating illness, Rose is tackling university.

Mary fled her home country in the middle of the night, carrying her infant son. She left behind her husband and the family that had hidden her from the militia in the days before her flight. The family she had stayed with was slaughtered the day after she fled. She made it to the United States and then to Canada, where she worked, studied, supported her family and friends, and patiently, gently tried to teach us about participatory learning and development. Things have improved now and she is able to move between her two countries, but her commitment to hearing all our voices remains strong.

I remember with awe some of the conversations I've heard at the Centre. I have watched a young feminist listen with respect while another young woman explains why she will wait for her parents to arrange a marriage for her. I have heard senior women explain the changes in their lives and immigrant women tell their stories of fear and joy. I have heard some women test their ideas on women's issues for the first time and others explore the issues of racism and homophobia. I have heard women from all backgrounds discuss the work that needs to be done to make Calgary a better place to live.

These conversations take place in the background, as other women work to find food for a family that has used their last visit to the food bank. To find bus tickets for a young woman who has her first job but no way to get there. To get a mother and her children to a shelter. To find self-esteem and parenting classes, support groups, legal advice, beds and furniture.

I've watched women share information, cooking, English, and computer skills. I've seen the woman who came into the Centre to use our fax machine stop to help another woman she'd never met write a resume. I've watched women listen with concern and sometimes horror, with joy and pride, to each other's stories.

And I've been proud to be associated with the Women's Centre and those many women, with their many stories.

A WARM FIRE
Anonymous

I have been in Canada for 15 years. I still feel like a new immigrant. This has happened to me all the time in my workplace and my daily life. My English is not good. When bad things happen to me, I panic.

One day I read in the Chinese newspaper an advertisement about the Practice English group at the Women's Centre and other activities. I called to register immediately.

I learn a lot of interesting things from the group. I meet a lot of friends from different backgrounds. My English has improved a lot. Whenever I come to the Women's Centre, I feel like I am back in my mother's arms. I feel comfortable and welcome.

My relationship with the Women's Centre is like a relationship with my mother, very close and dear. One day in April 1996 I was driving to work. All of a sudden another car hit me at the right-hand side. After the accident I was very scared, helpless, and frustrated. Both my mind and body suffered a lot. I went for assistance to the Women's Centre. All the staff members there are very caring. They helped me make a lot of phone calls to the insurance company and to lawyers and explained to me about any legal issues related to the car accident.

All this has helped me calm down. The Women's Centre is like a warm fire. It gives me a lot of comfort, support, and confidence. After the car accident I was very sick; I lost my ability to work and faced great financial difficulties. The Women's Centre gave me free food and grocery coupons and fed my family. My family of four is very grateful to the Centre, its staff members, and all the volunteers.

They also gave me a birthday present for my child. When my child received the birthday present, we all had tears in our eyes.

Canada is my second home. We came to Canada; we love Canada; we love the sincerity of the people and their passion. And this has all encouraged us to integrate into the Canadian society. I sincerely hope that the Women's Centre can work better and better in the future.

BEFRIENDING THE SELF
Marina Duke

My husband had a heart attack—he'd eaten his way clear up to 330 pounds! Both his parents died of heart conditions, but he must have thought he was immune. I had gone to Vancouver for a short holiday and after a few days our daughter phoned me with the news. I remember that my first thought was irrational but justified: "That man would do anything to keep me from enjoying myself!" I said I would come home when my holiday was finished, which I instantly paid for in the form of a huge, stress-related boil that grew from my hairline above my face. I stayed, wondering what I would be going back to. Would I be a widow or the wife of an invalid? How would I continue to live with someone I didn't love?

Upon arriving home I could sense that I was generally viewed as a heartless bitch for not coming to my husband's bedside when he could have died. My reaction to the situation came down to brutal honesty: I didn't want to come back so I didn't. A life-altering choice for all concerned. Our daughter took me to the hospital where my husband sat in bed feeling desperately sorry for himself. He had wept his plight to one of the nurses and he was a most unhappy man. Once he was home again, a pattern emerged consisting of no smoking and an extremely careful diet. Gradually he began to eat more and sneak a smoke at the side of the house. I have never smoked so I don't know the feelings involved, but I do know that I'd begun to hate him.

The hospital ran a very good cardiac program consisting of exercise, dietary advice, and sessions with a psychologist. They strongly suggested that the patients' partners join in on these sessions, which I did and my whole life changed. The doctor's intention was to try to determine what had caused the heart attack in the hope of avoiding another. My husband went to only a couple of these sessions, but the doctor invited me to continue and I did, for the best part of a year. In the course of our conversations, the psychologist found out I am an artist. He wanted to know what I was doing with my ability. When I replied "Not much!" he demanded to know why not. No one had ever cared enough to ask before.

I was embarking upon the intensely difficult and fascinating task of examining myself. I also did something that I later learned was quite typical—I fell in love with my therapist. I lived for Tuesday afternoons, and if an appointment was cancelled, I was devastated. I asked myself why this man could put me through such hell. I began to write poetry and buy myself lacy lingerie, and I went to our Tuesday appointments dressed as glamorously as if I'd been meeting a lover. I was 47 years old and feeling a passion I'd never experienced before in my life. Looking back, I believe that loving this man enabled me to do the work the situation required. Anything he could have suggested I would have seriously considered. I am thankful that he was both professional and respectful. At the end of one of our sessions, he told me that sometimes it was difficult for him too. It meant a great deal to me to finally know I wasn't struggling alone.

Slowly, steadily, he began to encourage me to seek out the artistic options that were available to me. I started by looking around the university, but I felt completely overwhelmed. Then I went to the art college and I thought I might just fit there. I made inquiries and I was told I needed to submit a portfolio consisting of photographic slides of my artwork and a written essay explaining why I wished to return to school at that point in my life. I applied. It seemed to take forever to hear from the college. I had two constant, conflicting thoughts: "What will I do if I'm not accepted and what will I do if I am?" The psychologist had asked me to call him when I heard the results. Being able to phone him and say that I'd been accepted at the Alberta College of Art was an extremely special moment in my life. By then it was spring. The doctor and I had been talking weekly since the previous summer and we needed to conclude our sessions. I had to say goodbye to this caring and sensitive man whom I had come to love deeply. I felt utterly dazed the day we parted. I don't cry easily, but during the following weeks, I wondered if I might just drown. Since I was still married, I shed my tears in private—in the bathtub and during long walks I took alone.

Those therapeutic sessions had begun to show me who I was beyond being a wife and mother. Upon entering college and becoming a part of the drawing program, what I needed became more evident with each new assignment. Sculpture, ceramics, hand-made paper, painting, collage, intense art history sessions, and written papers were both terrifying and intensely exciting. The first time I received an A, I was in heaven. I was raised in the era of Marilyn Monroe and the Barbie doll, and I had bought into the idea that I was pretty but stupid. Finding out that I had a fully functioning brain was a tremendous joy. I was fortunate to have some excellent teachers (I learned much from the bastards as well) and one of the best was my painting instructor. He is a very talented man and one of God's best works, a good teacher. I had never painted before, but I found I was producing work I was exceptionally proud of.

Upon finishing my third year, I realized I needed to see the ocean and headed once again for Vancouver. All the art I'd been creating was of such a personal nature that I was able to dive into my emotional problems. I knew I needed to leave my husband, as I no longer liked, respected, or trusted him. I walked around the sea wall dissecting my situation with the sound, scent, and sight of the water aiding me. By the time I returned home, I knew my marriage was over. I had been married for thirty years, and my husband, friends, and family assumed I would remain so indefinitely. It was a shock for all concerned to learn otherwise. I soon found a lawyer, an apartment, and a mover. I also began the monumental task of deciding what belonged to whom and what I would need to buy. After a fight with my husband, I sat in a downtown park trying to calm myself. I looked at the surrounding buildings and noticed a phone number in huge letters on the side of a high rise. I assumed I'd never be able to afford the place, but there was no harm in looking. I looked at the apartment, loved it, and found that I could afford it— for the time being.

Moving day came. I kissed the 21-year-old and the cat goodbye and rode downtown between my two movers in the cab of their van. I went to sleep that night with my boxes all around me, but I had everything where I wanted it within two days. I loved that apartment. I saw the sun come up in the east and sink behind the mountains in the west. There were hot air balloons, double rainbows, electric storms, snowstorms with flakes the size of torn paper, and eerie, mysterious fog. My apartment on the 38th floor faced south.

It took me two more years to finish college, and by then I'd also become a grandmother. I've never regretted the decision to leave my marriage and I know that my choices began when I learned to befriend myself.

I'VE COME A LONG WAY
Anonymous

I came to the Women's Centre by chance. I was a young university student thinking of going into the social sciences when a community worker in my doctor's office suggested that I come to volunteer at the Centre. I didn't know anything about the Centre and wasn't really sure that I wanted to volunteer, but since this woman told me I should, I did. Everybody was very nice, but I was scared about helping clients. I was young and insecure. That was six years ago and I've come a long way since then.

As I reflect on my life, I know that what I have done and who I am would be radically different if the Centre were not in my life. My exposure to, awareness of, and acceptance of different kinds of people are definitely a major part of this. Before coming to the Centre, I had never known anyone with a physical or mental disability, anyone who was a lesbian, anyone who was very rich, poor, or homeless, or anyone from different parts of the world.

On my first shift I met a woman who told me she had schizophrenia. We developed a good relationship, and I found out how schizophrenia affected every part of her life in terrible ways. She told me how her neighbors tried to control her mind by infiltrating her computer, and she often told me she was going to die that day because she had some terrible disease that was killing her. I was amazed at how completely she believed all those things and thought to myself how well she did to function from day to day, considering she thought the whole world was out to get her. She had had a career before becoming sick in her late twenties, and now she delivered fliers for a living. She had a great sense of loss about the life that she had led. I looked forward to our conversations. I eventually found out that she was a lesbian, and that her partner also had schizophrenia. I remember thinking how brave she was to live from day to day with the challenges of being a lesbian woman with schizophrenia, and I came to really admire her. She stopped coming to the Centre after awhile because her partner's schizophrenia grew worse. I called her sometimes, but eventually she was paranoid to the point where she wouldn't come to the Centre. When she lost her job, it seemed to me that she didn't get out of the house much. She stayed connected to the world through the Internet. I still think about her sometimes and wonder how she is doing.

I have met many different women at the Women's Centre and have heard many of their stories. Some of them are in this book, but most are not. A 15-year-old, pregnant woman whose mother had frozen in the cold and whose boyfriend was abusive. All she wanted was to be independent, but she was too young to qualify for social services, even though her legal guardians were alcoholics. I also met a homeless woman who hadn't eaten all day. I took her to a coffee shop across the street and bought her soup and a sandwich. I'll never forget the toothless smile on her face. Her brother was going to pick her up later that day to take her back home. And the woman from Southeast Asia who had grown up in South America. She spoke Spanish perfectly. Last thing I heard, she and her husband had a baby. And then there was the woman whose husband kidnapped their child and took her to Africa. More than ten years later, she has her daughter back and they are struggling to get to know each other.

So many stories, I could go on for a while. I can't even begin to describe how all these people have influenced me. So many of them have touched my heart in so many ways. I have developed an awareness of the struggles that women face here and in other parts of the world. I have developed a respect for the humanity and worth of all people, and I have learned the value of diversity. These qualities are integral to the person I am now, and I don't know how else I could have come to this point. The Women's Centre has allowed me to develop into a richer person, not by preaching or coaxing, but by creating a safe environment for women like me to be themselves, learn from each other, and support each other in their life struggles and development. It's quite amazing, and after all these years, sometimes I still can't believe the magic of this place.

I eventually felt safe and comfortable enough to admit what I had known for a long time—that I am a lesbian. This was a difficult thing for me to come to terms with, because it is such a taboo in my culture. Growing up, the only thing I learned about lesbians was that they were sick and looked like men because they wanted to be men. I certainly never met one. For a long time I thought I couldn't be a lesbian because I didn't want to be a man or dress like one. At the Women's Centre I got to know lesbians who looked like women, led "normal" lives, and were successful. What a concept! But it was still difficult because I didn't want to be a disappointment to my family. They are very important to me and I didn't want to lose them. It took me a while to come to terms with the fact that I could be a good person *and* a lesbian.

No one at the Centre thought it was a big deal that I am a lesbian. They accepted and supported me just as they always had. This continues to mean a great deal to me, because there aren't many places where you can feel normal even though you are "different." A lot of people try to pretend it isn't an issue for them, but I can tell that it is. My best friend felt like this. We had been best friends for years and had promised each other that we would always be friends. When I told her I was a lesbian, she said that it didn't matter to her, but she stopped calling me. I tried for awhile to keep in contact with her, but soon I stopped calling, and she never called me back. I was very hurt. A few years have passed, and I heard recently that she married the boyfriend she had when we were friends. I obviously wasn't invited. I think I'm more angry than hurt now.

It is very difficult to be a lesbian woman and even more difficult to be a lesbian couple in this society. You can't get legally recognized as a couple, and everyone at the hospital looks at you funny when you tell them your partner is your next of kin. My partner and I had to get personal directives to ensure that we can make decisions about each other in case something happens to one of us. I sometimes imagine how people I work with professionally would react if they knew I was a lesbian. I am pretty sure a lot of them wouldn't want to have anything to do with me anymore, and that is a harsh reality for me. It makes me very sad and angry, and I still wish my family could be proud of my long-term relationship with my partner just as they would be if I were married to a man. I love the Women's Centre because it accepts and celebrates difference. I will always be a part of the Women's Centre and the women of the Centre will always have a special place in my heart.

GROCERY GIRL
Elana Chin

"**C**hinky Chinky Chinaman!" These words rang loudly in my ears as I crossed the schoolyard to my debate club meeting. At the age of 13, I realized for the first time that, although I was born in Canada, I would always be considered Chinese before Canadian. When I looked at my black hair, almond-shaped eyes, and olive skin in the mirror, I recognized that I was different, but it never occurred to me that others also made those distinctions. The racial taunting was minimal, considering my circumstances. I was one of the few Chinese students in predominantly white, upper-middle-class schools in a fairly affluent neighbourhood. This neighbourhood had petitioned a Chinese family to move out in 1960, fearing that its presence would devalue property. We were one of the first Chinese families to move into that neighborhood and my parents still reside there after 26 years.

Up until high school, all my friends and acquaintances were white. So there were some moments when I suffered humiliation. But let's face it: kids can be cruel. Some children suffered because they wore glasses, others because they were fat, flat-chested, or short. I just happened to be Chinese. The trauma was short-lived, and for the most part, being Chinese made me feel not only different but also special.

I grew up in a multi-generational home with four other siblings, a Grandmother who ran the household, and parents who worked six days a week. We spoke Chinese at home until we started school, at which point English quickly became our language. My parents were always embarrassed about our inability to speak Chinese, although we still understood it. The proficiency with which my parents spoke and wrote English increased as my Chinese declined over the years. After being in Canada for over 40 years, my Grandmother still hadn't found much use for the English language, continually scolded us for speaking it in our home, and barely spoke a word of it herself. But she miraculously understood English when any of the children swore in her presence. The older I become, the more I regret that my parents didn't follow through with their threats of sending us to Chinese school. It saddens me to think that my children will not be able to communicate with their Great Grandmother, now 88 years old, as her stories are far more interesting than mine could ever be.

My parents owned a corner grocery store where we grew up and learned our work ethic. There was no getting around working in the store. I'll always remember the Sundays when my parents would divide all the shelves into five sections and we would each be assigned a section to dust and tidy. Then we had to move all the stock to the front of the shelf and make all the English labels face forward. I remember that job because it was the most mundane task that any child could do (next to dusting what seemed to be the largest fake orange tree in the world—a weekly job my Grandmother assigned at home). When we could count, we became cashiers. When we were tall enough, we packed groceries and when we were old enough to handle knives, we became butchers. I'm sure that we uttered many complaints, but we knew that this was our lot in life and there was no way around it. But it meant that we couldn't participate in extra-curricular activities, as our friends did.

In grade six I was one of the privileged few to become a school patrol. I had to decline the job because it took me away from the store when it was my duty to watch all the kids at lunch hour to ensure that they didn't walk off with three bags of cookies underneath their jackets. Being a patrol seemed like an important job at the time, but I guess my parents felt that keeping their profits was more important. When I declined the position, my teacher threw a chair at me in a fit of anger. The wrath of my parents, however, would have been far greater. It seemed unfair at the time when I knew that my friends had only to clean their rooms or take out the garbage. I must also confess that I was never proud that I was a grocery girl and that my parents were not professionals like most of my friends' parents.

I feel grateful now for all that they put me through. By watching my parents all those years, and by working in the grocery store alongside them, I learned the meaning of hard work and how not to be afraid of it. By my parents' standards, the worst kind of person is a lazy person. I respect and admire my parents for having been able to clothe, house, and educate five children. They immigrated to Canada for a better life and they made sacrifices so that their children could have a better life than they did. I'm happy to say that they have done well for all of us.

People have asked me if I am close to my parents and to that I have said, "As close to Chinese parents as one can get, I guess." What I mean is that my parents, like most Chinese parents I know, are not physically affectionate. They were not in the habit of kissing, hugging, or expressing their love verbally for any of us. But I knew that they loved me. They would express their love by making sure that my basic needs were met. They made sure that I was always clothed, housed, fed, and educated, and this made me feel secure. My parents never needed to tell me that they would be there for me because that went without saying. Talk of a personal nature wasn't common between the parents and children in my family. We didn't talk about "the birds and the bees," menstruation, boyfriends, or life aspirations. Yet I don't feel as though I've missed out on anything. I do periodically tell my parents and my Grandmother now that I love them, which causes them to blush a little. They never say "I love you" back, but they may nod their heads and say "mm" in acknowledgment.

The adolescent years are often considered turbulent years; as a

17

Chinese adolescent girl, I also had to deal with cultural issues. Like most teenagers, I went through a phase where developing independence and self-identity was important to me. My parents never let me forget that being Chinese was part of my identity. It was a struggle at times to integrate the Canadian culture that I knew and the Chinese culture that my parents knew. Most of my friends at school were white, but outside of school I attended Chinese dances, played volleyball for Chinese teams, and joined Chinese clubs. I was never discouraged from having white friends, but I certainly wasn't encouraged. In my younger teen years, it never occurred to me that I would be a part of any community other than the Chinese one. I always thought that I would take part in Chinese circles with Chinese friends and someday be married to a Chinese man.

Conflict began when I was in high school and I met my first love. He was kind, funny, honest, and bright, but none of that mattered to my parents because he wasn't Chinese. I never introduced him to my parents and we never talked about him, but this is when all the discord began. They started to listen in on my phone calls and follow me around, so it became quite a sneaky affair. There was plenty of tension, many tears on my part, and some blowups in which my Father would inevitably say, "What would your children look like?" He was implying, of course, that any offspring of interracial copulation would be a mutant freak. Another line my parents would use was: "Do you want to be divorced? Don't you know that most white people get divorced?" They stopped saying that after my oldest brother married a Chinese woman and divorced within a year and a half.

After about a year of all this fighting at home, I couldn't deal with the stress any more. I sacrificed my relationship for some peace at home. I knew that I was too young to be out on my own and decided that while I lived at home I would respect my parents' rules, but I didn't respect their deep-seeded prejudice against any race other than their own. Not that they really had anything against white people, they just didn't want one in the family. In the years to follow, I dated a Chinese man of whom my parents approved. Mind you, the only criteria they had was that he be Chinese. My parents only wanted what was best for me, and that didn't include a white husband.

I eventually finished my undergraduate degree in Education, taught in Fiji and Japan, and returned to Edmonton to supply teach. Within a year of my return, my Mother became ill with lupus and couldn't work in the grocery store. Although two of my brothers lived in the city at the time, I had to quit teaching to help run the store because my Father couldn't do it alone. It was never openly stated that I should be the one to make the sacrifice, but I knew my parents felt that my career aspirations (no matter what they were) could never be as important as my brothers' careers; I would just be married off to another family and be supported. That is not to say that my parents didn't want me to have an education, because they expected us all to complete university, including the daughters. So there I was—a grocery girl once more—until we decided to sell the business. At that point, I went out East to do postgraduate work and stayed there to work in community development.

Once I moved away from home, my personal life picked up. I was finally able to become involved in relationships without having a dark cloud over my head. Feeling as though I had just been released from prison, I dated like a fiend for about a year and then met my husband with whom I now have two children. No, my husband is not Chinese. No, we are not divorced. Yes, my children are beautiful. And yes, my parents both accept and love my husband. Why did my parents have a change of heart? To be honest, I'm not really sure. I've never asked them about it and they've never volunteered to talk about it. It could be because they realized that they no longer have control over my life. I think they were also affected by my eldest brother's divorce. Two of my siblings are in mixed marriages, so I'm no longer the "black sheep" of the family. I also think that my parents are able to get past the race issue and see that my husband is good, kind, bright, and hard working. I recognize that seeing past the "colour" was a big step for my parents and for my Grandmother. I understand that this evolutionary process was not easy for them either, which makes me have all the more faith in people and their ability to change.

WALKING INTO A HUG
Anonymous

Several weeks ago, in the midst of a severe crisis involving my battle with chronic depression, I stumbled into the Women's Centre and it was like walking into a hug. I was immediately made welcome and offered coffee, cookies, and conversation. I looked around numbly at the warm quilts and creative masks on the walls, the plants scattered around, and the wonderful women quietly talking and laughing.

I sat in a comfortable chair and browsed through the many pamphlets, brochures, and courses that were related to the issues I was facing. Through exposure to this information (that, even though I am a teacher, I had no idea existed), I was able to begin the essential work in my process of healing. I was also offered use of the Internet to keep in touch with special friends via e-mail—something I had desperately needed to do.

Now I have joined several support groups; I have a great therapist, a good doctor, and new friends here at the Centre, and I am able to express my gratitude by occasionally volunteering (without any pressure or expectations).

In our busy, often impersonal city, how blessed we are to have the Women's Centre to support, nurture, and inform women from all walks of life.

Thank you, Women's Centre…for everything!

THE SUMMER OF '97: A SUCCESS STORY
Yvonne Stanford

It all started with a phone call from Susan. The Women's Resource Centre was being closed at the end of the month. No consultation with staff, volunteers, clients, referring agencies, or the women of Calgary. Just a notice of closure.

Should we fight back? Should we protest? Or should we accept the inevitable? "I'm in if you're in," we said to one another. We decided to call a meeting of supporters to see if, together, we could find a way to save the Centre. We decided on June 6, 1997—one week away.

Narmin Ismail-Teja, facilitator extraordinaire, agreed to co-facilitate this meeting with me—and the angry, energized volunteers of the Centre swung into action, spreading the news, requesting attendance and support.

On June 6 in the Carpenters Union Hall, over 50 women one by one spoke about what the Women's Resource Centre meant to them and to the women of Calgary. We formed the Women's Resource Centre Action Coalition, which grew to 50 organizations and over 300 individual members in the next few weeks.

All the staff and all the volunteers of the Centre dedicated themselves to the work of the Action Coalition. We called a second community meeting, with a broader audience including funders, for June 26. Amal Umar, of the highest credibility and stature in the community, agreed to co-chair this meeting with me.

On the afternoon of June 26 a glorious diversity of women filled the Carpenters Union Hall: women speaking in a variety of languages; immigrant women and Canadian-born women; women with disabilities and able-bodied women; women who had come to the Centre in need and had stayed to help; women representing other agencies who understood the importance of the program; poor women and rich women; white women and women of colour; women with long years of experience in organizing and women who had never before defined themselves as activists. The United Way and Family and Community Support Services (FCSS), the past funders of the Resource Centre, sent representatives. Hazel Gillespie from Petro-Canada came to listen. Gary Dickson, MLA, attended and promised his support. And once again, one by one, women introduced themselves and told the story of the Women's Centre.

We called a meeting for July 9, asking supporters to come together to decide what to do next. We prepared a continuum of possibilities for what we could do, ranging from disbanding our coalition to continuing to organize for a fully funded and independent centre. The Centre was closed, our clients were confused and possibly lost, and the YWCA had given up the lease on the Resource Centre's space on 10th Street. We were tired and overworked.

I remember driving into this meeting from the country, knowing how scarce our resources were, how overworked our volunteers were, how many women's centres across Canada had closed, how many programs had been cut, and how high the barriers were. It was a lovely summer's day—I wondered how many would be at the meeting. Could we make a decision about our future that would leave us feeling good about what we believed in and proud of our efforts?

I walked into a meeting room full of energized and determined women. In the go-round, each woman in turn voiced her support to organize a fully funded, independent Women's Centre and committed her time and energy to make it happen.

"My baby is due in October, but I'm in until my contractions

23

start."

"I'm working three jobs this summer to go back to school in the fall, but count me in."

"I'm away for two weeks, but I can work for the rest of the summer."

"This isn't how I planned to spend this summer, but this is important."

Key leaders were there, or had sent word. I was overwhelmed with the passion, the anger, the commitment, and the determination not to lose our Centre. We chose to go for it—to find a way to reopen our Centre.

I thought we were working at breakneck speed and accomplishing so much. But Maria reminded me all summer that we needed to go faster—the women in her sewing group were waiting, and women who needed the Centre had no other place to go for help.

We put out a call for support, asking for membership in the Action Coalition, donations for expenses, startup funds and ongoing support. We said:

> *We are determined to see a Women's Resource Centre that offers supportive information and referral, peer counseling, personal development groups and workshops, a legal advice clinic, emergency and crisis support, and advocacy. We are determined to offer a holistic service, assisting diverse constituencies of women to identify their needs and to access the broad range of community resources. We will offer a connection to community, especially for immigrant women building first links to mainstream Canadian society, and for mainstream and minority women isolated in crises.*

We decided that we would not reopen the Centre until we had adequate funds and promises to start up and operate at least until the end of 1998. We would not open tenuously, with the risk of closure and further disruption for our clients. We said:

> *The Action Coalition believes that our vision for a Women's Resource Centre is a unique and necessary service to the women of Calgary and must continue with adequate funding for staff and programming.*

The United Way agreed to a meeting with us on August 7. We wrote a business plan. We drew up a budget. Donations in dollars, pledges, and in-kind were coming in. Hazel Gillespie, National Community Investment Manager from Petro-Canada, came to the meeting to state her belief in and support for the Centre. Oxfam agreed to provide us with an organizational home, as well as institutional support and charitable tax status for donations.

We opened negotiations with Calholme to renew or extend the lease on the 10th Street space. We gathered in our political support, municipally and provincially. We told our story, explaining that we offered a unique service to an under-resourced constituency. Our writers and poets found the words. We insisted on the Endowment Fund that had been set up, while a part of the YWCA remain with this program. We lamented the resources that we needed—the pamphlets and books and furniture—that were in storage at the YWCA. We found new supporters: the Calgary Foundation, the Junior League, and individual women and their families.

I remember making a call to Sheila O'Brien, Vice-President at Nova and a long-time activist and supporter of women. I had prepared myself for a careful but passionate, committed but not angry, needy but not blaming appeal for her help in getting this corporate support. Sheila was on board before I started. She knew about our program and how important it was. Nova was in, matching Petro-Canada's commitment for $10,000 in each of two years.

The evening before a September 12 Action Coalition meeting, I tallied up our committed funding support. We were to make a stop/ go decision on reopening and we needed to know that we could sustain the Centre. The staff and all the volunteers—over 100 of them—were committed to working with an independent Centre. Calholme had agreed to a four-month lease on the 10th Street location and had promised to help us find another space if it we had to move. The United Way had committed funds on a pilot project basis to the end of 1999, with extra funds for an extensive community evaluation. In-kind donations helped to reduce our estimated expenditures. We had some promises for fund-raising events. The entire Endowment Fund committee had become our fund-raising committee. We were close, but not quite there. My phone rang, with a generous donation of $5,000 to start up and $5,000 in 1998 from the family of a long-time volunteer. My doorbell rang, with a family promising an ongoing monthly donation of $100. We could do it!

On September 12 the Action Coalition made the decision to reopen the Women's Resource Centre under the name the Women's Centre. We were invited to celebrate our monumental victory at a traditional Women's Centre potluck at Jennifer and Julie's on October 7. The Centre reopened on October 15, 1997.

In the summer of '97 a community of women and men who believed in a vision of a women's space and essential services for women worked together to make it happen. The Women's Centre exists today because of them.

PLAIN LANGUAGE
Loraine Luterbach

My name is Loraine. I'm the one who talks too much! I first heard about the Women's Centre when it was part of the YWCA. My friend Janet asked me if I would like to do some plain language translation work with her and some other women. This was for a project for both the Women's Centre and the Vocational and Rehabilitation Research Institute (VRRI). We wanted to write easy-to-read information for women. The Women's Centre told us what information they wanted and we did the work together. I am a woman with a developmental disability and sometimes I find things hard to read. I think it helps me to think about easier words when I work with a group. When we make things easier to read, it helps many people. I am really happy that I can help other people when they find it hard to read. It makes me feel good when I'm busy with those projects.

I worked with our plain language groups on the Mary Dover House rental agreement, so that people who wanted to live there knew what the rules were. In the rental form they gave us, some of the words were very hard to understand, so we changed them. Now every person who lives in the Mary Dover House uses the form we wrote.

After that, we made five pamphlets about separation and divorce. We also wrote a pamphlet to help people understand what happens if they shoplift. I feel really great when people read the pamphlets. I am helping myself then, and helping others too. I like to feel needed.

At this time the YWCA said there would be no more funding

for the Women's Resource Centre. I felt sad. I didn't want them to close it down, because where else could people go? They can't just be out on the street.

I went with my friends to a meeting to tell people why I wanted the Women's Centre to stay open. There were a lot of people there. I told everyone why the Women's Centre was important to me. I am very happy that the new Women's Centre has opened. All the people who work there are very nice. It helps to have good people to work with.

One of the best things about the Women's Centre is the pot-luck dinners. There is a lot of good food. I remember a pasta salad with ham in it and chicken wings. There were buns and pickles and juice. I took brownies I made myself. They disappeared fast. A lot of people came to the pot-lucks and everybody brought something. Sometimes the food is different because people come from other countries. I like to meet new people. Then I can learn more for myself and I can tell them what I do. One time I was able to tell people I had a job interview to go to in England. They were very surprised. At first I thought it was all a dream. I didn't get the job, but it was fun to go and I met my pen pal in Wales for the first time.

The best pot-luck was at Susan's house. This was a party because we had been told that the Women's Centre could carry on. I met a lot of nice people. I like it when people listen to my stories. Sometimes people don't listen to me because I have a disability. I wish we could have more people listen and then there wouldn't be arguments. One person I met had an e-mail address. I was learning to use the Internet, so I wrote to her later when she moved to the USA and she wrote back. Now she does not have that e-mail address and I don't know where she is.

Because of the Women's Centre/VRRI project, I was able to go to a conference in New York. I told people there about plain language, why it was important, and how to write it. I told them it might take us a little bit longer to do the work because we have a disability, but we get there in the end. A lot of people came to our session and took the pamphlets and my business cards. I bought some postcards and a key chain for my friend, Sandra (who couldn't come with us), and I went to the museum.

I still do plain language work. All of us in the translation groups have learned a lot about how to do it. We write useful stuff about how to be safe on a date, about guardianship and trustees for people with developmental disabilities, and about health issues like diabetes. I want to do a lot more of it. I am glad we got to work with people at the Women's Centre.

IMAGES
Valerie G. Connell

Wimmin are the colour, texture, and fabric of a glorious tapestry, and the Women's Centre provides the opportunity to experience a living tapestry that is always changing. Support, laughter, community, diversity, and commitment to justice come to my mind when I think of the Women's Centre in Calgary. For me the image that fits best is that of oasis: an oasis from the storm, an oasis in the desert.

I came to Calgary at the end of August 1998 to take a two-year Journalism Arts course at the Southern Alberta Institute of Technology. I have not-so-good memories of living here years ago. It took a good deal of courage to come back.

Returning to school was scary. Could I do it? Was I nuts at my age, 55, to go back to school? Would I get a job when I finished to pay back the student loan that I had to get? I had all kinds of fears.

The realization that I would be entering a very patriarchal environment was a consideration for me when I decided to come to Calgary. I have spent much time and energy over the past several years unlearning unhealthy attitudes and practices I accumulated living as a womyn in a very patriarchal environment.

Early on one of my instructors told me about the Women's Centre in Calgary and gave me the phone number. What a gift that was and continues to be. I have volunteered at the Women's Centre for over a year. The days I come here are an oasis experience for me.

I recently did a three-week practicum at the *Calgary Sun* and was able to adjust my time so that I could keep my "Thursdays" at the Women's Centre. Now I am doing a public-relations practicum at the Women's Centre. It's a joy to spend the day among wimmin.

Coming to the Women's Centre is like a cool breeze on a hot, sticky day or a warm fire on a cold, windy night.

I Am a Beautiful Woman
Tanis Castillo

Sometime in September 1999 I was, as usual, having difficulty in my life trying to be independent. I am a Treaty Blackfoot Native from Gleichen, Alberta. I have had nothing but negativity and mean behaviour lashed out on me all my life. I'm 33 years old, attractive, educated, determined, and at times mouthy. I'm lucky to still be alive. In my life I have seen a lot of horrible things that get pushed under the carpet by people. There is a HUGE problem with hate in Calgary. People hate each other so much. If you're an Indian woman, you haven't got a chance. That's the truth!

I'm an Indian. I knew nobody would help me. I was starting more courses at Mount Royal College. My now ex-common-law partner was not happy that I couldn't help out. "Nobody hires Indians or wants an Indian at their front counter or desk," he told me. Just like all the relationships I try to have, it was the same deal. The man supports me, I try to get a job. I take course after course. Nothing. Then the financial burden falls on my partner, arguments arise, and I am abused mentally, emotionally, spiritually, and physically. It's just terrible. I really feel like I don't have a chance.

My ex had a female friend. She pretended to love Natives, but deep down she couldn't stand me because I would stand up for myself. She would tell my partner and others things like "You will have a crappy life with Tanis because she's Indian. She's just like all the other Natives. They sit at home and collect welfare and never get anywhere." This would trouble my partner because he had deep feelings for me. Just like the others, he would get abusive over money and over what other people thought about Indians.

I'm so tired and overcome by the discrimination I face every day. I cry and cry. I've lost my children. My parents lost their children, their parents lost their children, and it's all because we don't have a chance. In court or in life. That's the truth. Don't let anyone underestimate this HUGE, TERRIBLE PROBLEM.

Anyway I refused to be kept down. I collected Welfare at 10th Avenue SW. They call it "Native Welfare." There's a Native woman at the front, but your worker is white and hates you. At least mine did. She found out I had my son with me at times. He goes back and forth between me and his father, who does his best not to tolerate discrimination (God Bless Him). He has watched me suffer and go to Court for years—to be charged for things I never did—and lose court cases for custody of my son Jordan, who is now eight years old.

I'm trying to keep my story simple, but it is NOT. I am an endangered species. I must plan what I am going to do. So I went to the Women's Centre, scared that they would do something to harm me. I didn't have a phone. I can't get a job to pay for a phone or any other things the average white family has. So I used the phone at the Centre. I wanted to charge my ex for abusing me and also charge his female friend for coaching him on how to abuse Native women. I was devastated about losing another relationship because of hate and discrimination like so many times before. Let me tell you it doesn't get easier.

The women at the Centre helped me to prepare statements and collect evidence against these abusive people. It's hard to charge someone you had planned to be with for the rest of your life. I had to get a restraining order too. The women supported me through all the time and effort it takes to do these things. I even became brave enough to bring my son out from hiding and I brought him to the Centre. They were so nice to him I was choked up with tears. It's hard to find people you can trust who won't call the welfare department on you because you're having a happy life. My son watched a video while I did up my resume.

I get very lonely and feel like there is no sense in looking for work or going back for more education. I go to the Centre and I feel like I can go on. I guess you could say the women at the Centre saved my life many times by letting me use the phone to call the food bank or doctors or two good friends: Yvette, and the only lady who ever gave me a job, Linda. She saved my life a couple of times too (God Bless Her) and has given me the courage and the strength not to give up. She is a white woman, but she loves me. I will always remember the people who have helped me. They are so few and far between.

I always go that extra bit further to prove my point. I am a beautiful woman. I am healthy in every way. I do not drink alcohol, or live on a street corner anymore, or do cocaine to ease the pain of being an Indian. Eight years now and I'm still being stopped everywhere I turn. Homes, jobs, even my son. I know the social workers are stressed but they are keeping families apart as we speak. But not my little Jerrod, who is five, and who I am hiding. I see him a lot, but if I collect welfare they will find some petty flaw and make a case to keep him from me, as they have done with thousands of other Canadians, especially in Alberta and BC. The United Nations says it is illegal to keep children from their mothers. Child Welfare does it all the time. There is no chance against Child Welfare. The judges believe what they say, and the parents have no rights. We're supposed to, but we really don't. I pray every day this silent murder will stop. It's wrong to kill people from the inside out. Give back all the children to their families—to their mothers—and I promise you hate, crime, and alcohol and drug abuse will diminish.

Thank you the women at the Centre! We all help each other. One time the senior co-ordinator gave me tickets to see the Calgary

Philharmonic Orchestra. I'm still quite moved by what I saw. I had never seen anything so beautiful. I love to dance and play music. I have one year of piano lessons. When and if I ever am given a chance to work, I'm going to continue my piano lessons. I know how. I need a chance. I need the Centre! So does my son! He needs to know that not everyone is mean and hateful. Jessica, Susan, Magdalen, and all the other ladies I met: God Bless and don't give up! Lives are at stake. I need good role models like you. Many thanks and love always.

REFLECTION ON CHARITABLE STATUS
Mary Valentich

The words "charitable status" make me cringe. Because I am a social worker, one might expect me to be more favourably inclined to this term. Perhaps it is *because* I am a social worker that I so dislike the words, knowing that they hark back to an era when "good works" were the order of the day for the wealthy classes who could afford to be kind and generous to those less fortunate. But there is another, more personal reason for my distaste: I recall my mother telling me that one December a Christmas hamper arrived at our door, offered by a representative of one of the local Catholic societies. With barely contained annoyance, my working-class mother declined the turkey and the trimmings; she and my Dad would provide Christmas dinner as they always had. She was offended at having achieved "charitable status" in the eyes of well-meaning people she considered her equals. She and her family were not "less than."

When I became a board member of the Women's Centre last year, I learned that the organization had applied for charitable status in order to gain various tax benefits. I was not aware of the machinations necessary to refine our agency's statement of purpose and philosophy to attain congruence with the federal government's decree regarding the nature of organizations deemed to have charitable status. I was negatively biased toward the term "charity" because it still conveyed "doing good" for people who are entitled, in my view, to various societal benefits simply because they are human and live in a country with abundant resources. I read a column in *The Globe and Mail* that expressed similar concerns to my own about the restrictions inherent in the government's designation of charitable status. Regrettably, I cannot recall the name of the woman who wrote this marvelous piece. I also read, with a degree of amusement, a *Calgary Herald* article decrying the restrictions of the government designation. In the *Herald's* view, however, the "right wing" organizations were deemed ineligible while all the "left wing" groups were being granted charitable status almost automatically. The latter organizations were reaping all sorts of benefits denied to the former organizations, which the newspaper presumably supported. I couldn't quite accept that I might actually be agreeing, even in part, with a *Calgary Herald* editorial during this era of troubled *Calgary Herald* management/union relationships.

What bothers me about social agencies being designated as having charitable status? First, almost any procedure or process that involves government requires a lawyer or an accountant to manage it. Some of us, despite our advanced education, can no longer cope with complicated income tax forms that leave us bewildered as to what we should pay and why. It is not surprising that lawyers are needed to process the complexities of government forms and government regulations as, undoubtedly, their colleagues are responsible for drafting these same forms and regulations. I do not mean to criticize competent and non-avaricious lawyers, many of whom perform "charitable" works that truly serve justice. But our society is increasingly lawyer-reliant and we cannot work our way through what should be "normal" processes and procedures using our expertise in human relationships and communication.

My second reason for resenting the designation of charitable status is that the Canadian government is implementing a very conservative ideology based on the premise that society ought to, and will continue to, consist of the "haves" and the "have-nots." Those of us who "have" are good folks who can volunteer our times in various ways. The typical charitable organization survives through the energy and ingenuity of devoted volunteers who maintain an underpaid and overworked staff. Maybe someday the banks and the major corporations will staff themselves primarily with people who love to donate their time to foster money-making and the rest of us can get salaries and commissions in the six figures. But I digress.

I would not be so upset with volunteers, most of whom are women, doing much of the necessary, socially oriented tasks that prevent the development of emotional, mental, and social problems if we could freely devote ourselves to working on more fundamental issues. It's one thing to advocate on behalf of one client experiencing a difficulty with a corporation or a government organization. What if several clients are experiencing similar problems? What if there are persons, who are not clients, who would readily join in collective action to bring about legislative or institutional social change?

STOP says Big Bro. You used some "bad words." Collective action, social change...That is a political stance. You may be putting your "charitable" organization in jeopardy. Remember, we like the status quo because it keeps order in the society. No furor, no nasty demonstrations, no protests and NO CHANGE. With the status quo in place, the same people can keep economic and political power and the rest can struggle on. It's always been that way and so it should continue. So what if you do "feminist social work", which involves a structural analysis that questions how the social systems that are in place may be contributing to the problems? We don't want to hear about that nasty political stuff!

Guess what, Big Bro and whoever supports you. You are just as heavily engaged in political action by maintaining the status quo. But you don't wish to see it. You are mainly concerned with ensuring that countless volunteers across the country keep on providing basic social necessities to the poor, to the disabled and the elderly, to newcomers, and to Aboriginal peoples. You have little interest in enabling people to take charge of their own lives, except in limited, individualistic ways. It's fine to help an unemployed person to find a job, but it is not fine to lobby the government for more English as a Second

Language classes so that newcomers are not discriminated against in their job searches. I could think of many examples of this short-sighted attitude, but I prefer to think of how I can change our political system, rather than simply vote one group out and another in. This is how to say NO to a money-grubbing, highly individualistic, competitive society that shuns those who follow a different drummer and cares little for equity for all.

ALTERNATIVE LIVING
Anonymous

The way the Women's Centre helped me when I was homeless was to give me a place to go. Homeless means no home. Sometimes I had a lot of time with no place to go.

I would leave the Mustard Seed at 8:00 AM. The Women's Centre did not open until 9:30 AM. I was never there at 9:30 but it gave me a place when I did come.

After leaving the Seed I usually went to the Drop In Centre. Their day services would open at 8:00 AM. I would want a shower. Each person puts her name on a list and waits her turn. By the time I had my shower it was close to 10:00. The D.I. is a haven for smokers, but I do not smoke and I am allergic to cigarette smoke, so I never stayed long. When I got to the Centre I could have a cup of coffee. I only drink decaf (another one of my quirks). If I was hungry I would munch and munch and munch. Having an appetite is not a problem when you are homeless—I got a lot of exercise.

The Women's Centre provided me with an address and telephone number. Both the Seed and D.I. provide the same service but both are overflowing. The Centre also provided me with a computer and fax machine to work on. D.I. has both, but only staff members are allowed to use them.

One of the things I did daily was sleep. It's very hard to sleep at the shelter. I stayed overnight once at the D.I. (don't do that; intoxicated people come in all night). The Mustard Seed was different. I would line up for my bed at 8:00 PM. I liked to be first because the Seed would allow people to smoke between 9:30 and 10:00.

After going to our lockers, we didn't start to settle down until close to 10:30 PM. My bed was a mat on a concrete floor. It was very difficult to sleep when I was sharing a room with at least 70 people. Women have a separate section, but that did not matter. I heard the whole room. If someone beside me was sick, well, tough luck.

Another reason for lack of sleep was theft. I always felt that if I slept deeply enough someone would rob me blind. There is absolutely no basis for that assumption. At both the D.I. and the Seed I would line up. Line up for tea, line up for my meal, line up, line up, line up. I would leave everything behind at my table. My backpack with my purse in it and everything else I had on me. Nothing was ever stolen. Nothing. Once I lost my watch, but another lady found it and returned my watch to me a couple of days later. Does any of this knowledge mean anything at 11:00 PM when I am trying to sleep? Not a thing.

So I would go to the Women's Centre and sleep. There were five or six people there at the most. Some new people but at least half who I have known for years. I would sit on the couch or chair, get comfortable, and sleep for about an hour.

The Centre has a conference room. It's not available very often, but sometimes I was able to go in there. On those lucky days I could shut the door and be alone. Not very often, not for very long, but it was nice. It was the only time during the day (except for my shower) when I was alone. I could have my own space. Everything else was public. The washrooms are public, meals are public, and sleep is public.

While I was homeless, I decided I wanted to start a business. One of the ladies at the Centre helped me with a name. The Women's Centre provides people to take messages, faxes, and mail for me. Then there were business cards. The only paper I could afford to buy did not like the printer or vice versa. Susan and I worked on that problem and we won.

K & L's Big Adventure
Anonymous

Most of the time I think that my partner and I lead quiet, even boring lives. This September we will have been together 22 years. We are parents of a young son just entering adolescence. We check every evening to make sure his homework is completed. We don't go to bars, and most Friday evenings we watch videos with our son. We facilitate a parents' group once a month. Quiet, boring lives. Then there are those times when life is not so quiet, not so boring. Like the last four years. But I will have to jump back 16 years so that you can understand the last few.

My partner and I are lesbian mothers, and the parents' group we facilitate is a lesbian parents' group. These days, a lesbian mother is not such an unusual occurrence. Easier access to alternative fertilization has allowed lesbian women to create families. Babies are popping up all over the place. A virtual gayby boom.

But 16 years ago, when we decided to become parents, all the lesbian women we knew with children had come out of hetero-sexual relationships. At that time, the infertility clinic in Calgary was not even accepting single heterosexual women, let alone lesbian women, for insemination. Physicians in Alberta could not accept sperm in their offices, so the sperm banks in the United States that were willing to ship to Canadian lesbians were of no use to us. When we approached my partner's doctor, he told her to stand on the hookers' stroll and she'd get pregnant soon enough. We dropped him like a hot potato.

We did have a couple of gay male friends who had been in a

monogamous relationship for 15 years or so, and they donated once for us. My partner didn't become pregnant, and we decided to not use them again. They were becoming much too interested in the prospect of fathering a child, and the reason we had decided to go with insemination is that we didn't want a third party involved in the parenting of our child.

A friend of a friend told us that she knew some feminists who were married and who had decided that it was time that their husbands put up (out?) or shut up. She acted as a go-between so that the men did not know who they were helping, and we did not know who was the potential father. We used donors alternate evenings four times a month. When it was time to inseminate, we would phone the go-between, and she would drive over to the donor's house to pick up the sterilized container. We would drive to her house and park in the front. When she returned, she would give us the sample in a brown paper bag, and we would stuff it into a wool sock to keep it warm. Then we would drive home and inseminate.

It took six months of inseminations, but finally the two of us were gaping in disbelief at a positive home pregnancy test. Our son was probably the most planned child in the world. An uneventful nine months (and a few extra days) later, we had our son. Phase two of our big adventure had begun!

Our first challenge was to get our son's last name hyphenated with both our last names. We had given him my last name as a middle name, but we wanted to hyphenate both last names to reflect our role as parents. At the hospital, we put the hyphenated name on the birth registration, but it came back with a note saying that it couldn't be done. Although there was no policy on the books that said we couldn't, there was no policy to say that we could, and because there was no policy to say we could, we couldn't. Are you with me so far? There was a procedure for applying to implement a new policy, but the deadline had just passed and would not come up again for review for another few years. We were nothing if not persistent, however, and after speaking with the Minister of Health, who was also in charge of Vital Statistics, my partner applied for a name change. She changed her last name to the hyphenated name. Then she changed our son's name to the hyphenated name. A month later, she changed her name back, but left our son's. All that for a simple hyphen. Bureaucracy at its finest.

I'll skip over the next few years. I won't mention how we successfully lobbied to get the City of Calgary to change its definition of family to household so that lesbian and gay families could get into city recreational facilities as a family. I won't mention how a brave United Church minister created a new baptismal certificate to reflect our family, and how the congregation gaped as we stood, along with three heterosexual families, at the front of the church to have our son baptized, while thirteen lesbian friends grinned from the congregation. I won't mention how we started a private adoption when our son was 14 months old, but kept running into too many barriers, both legal and financial, to continue the process. I won't mention how, after 13 years employed with the same company, I was fired the morning after I appeared on the television news speaking about being a lesbian parent. I won't mention any of that.

What I will mention is the incident that provided the impetus for me to apply to adopt our son as a step-parent. I would pick him up in the afternoon from day care. One day, the day care telephoned to say that he had been hit in the back of the neck with a baseball bat that one of the children had brought to the school. When I arrived, he had difficulty moving his head, so I took him to the Children's Hospital. After filling out all the appropriate forms, I was informed that a doctor couldn't see him until his "real" mother came in to authorize any treatment. Because I wasn't recognized as his parent, he could have been forced to suffer until his biological parent came. This provided us with the push to renew our quest for adoption.

Up to that point, no same-sex second-parent adoptions had been successful in Canada. There was no case law on which to base a challenge. One lawyer suggested I try to obtain shared legal guardianship. That at least would allow me sign any documents that a parent could sign in any situation: medical, legal, or educational. We went to Family Court, filled out the required documents, served Social Services with the intent to obtain guardianship, and waited the required month before going to court. At that time, the process was free and did not require a lawyer.

We were fortunate in having the Chief Justice of Alberta Family Court, quite a liberal man, presiding that day. We sat in a courtroom crowded with lawyers and their clients. My partner and I sat through case after case of nasty custody battles, accusations of child abuse, and applications by Social Services to apprehend children who were considered a danger to themselves. We were appalled and saddened at what we heard. Just before the Court adjourned for lunch, the Court Clerk told us that they were ready to hear a happy case and that we would be up next.

When we stood before the judge, he said very little, paging slowly back and forth through our application. He asked a few brief questions, inspected the application one more time, and then, saying that he couldn't see why it would not be in our son's best interest, granted the guardianship application. We were extremely happy. This was the closest to adoption that we could come at the time. Yet it was not the same as adoption. I wanted to be a legal parent. We wanted to be a family under law.

In 1995, we heard some wonderful news out of Ontario. Four lesbian couples, each with a child conceived by alternative fertilization, had gone to court, asking that the partners of the biological mothers be allowed to second-parent adopt their partners' children. In the Ontario adoption legislation, the word "spouse" was defined as heterosexual, preventing the partners of lesbian mothers from adopting their children. The judge felt that the legislation violated the Charter of Rights, ordered the wording changed, and granted the adoptions.

This was precisely the case law that we were looking for. Although an Alberta judge would not be obligated to follow the ruling of an Ontario court, the case provided the kinds of arguments that we wanted to make. We thought our case would be easier, as the word "spouse" was not defined in the Child Welfare Act in Alberta, and we would not be forced to fight an already legislated heterosexual definition.

In July of 1995, we approached a law firm known for its commitment to the lesbian and gay community of Calgary. Both our lawyers, Gary and Sam (Sandra), were cautiously excited by the prospect of the case, but needed to do some research before they were willing to evaluate our chances of success.

By November, the two lawyers had done enough preliminary research to feel that we should be able to proceed with a successful adoption application. There was nothing in the Child Welfare Act stating that lesbians and gays could not adopt. We wanted to do a second-parent or step-parent adoption, because that was the only way that I could adopt our son without my partner losing her maternal rights. We were in a committed long-term relationship, our son had been born within our relationship, and there was no known father to complicate things legally.

Because there is strength in numbers, we approached another couple, also in a long-term relationship, who had a four-year-old son by alternative fertilization. They too were excited by the prospect, and in April of 1996 we began the adoption procedure. We decided to arrange home studies of both families. We contacted the lawyers from the Ontario case and all their expert witnesses. We wanted updated affidavits to support our contention that lesbian parents are just as fit as heterosexual parents and that children raised in lesbian families suffer no ill effects.

It took almost a year and a half to collect all the updated affidavits. We started the home studies in the spring of 1997. First my partner and I met for two hours in the office of the psychologist who was conducting the home study. Over the following weeks, we met with her separately for several interviews and wrote several lengthy and rather mystifying psychological and parenting assessment tests. Then our son met with her for a few hours and later took some tests. We returned as a family and spent some time in her office playroom under observation, playing with our son and the toys in the room. After that, she came out to our house, inspected the physical layout, and then observed us for an hour or so as we played some games.

By October of 1997 we finally had the psychologist's report, and we were very pleased with her findings. We were good parents, and our son was developing quite normally. By that time we also had the three expert affidavits in hand, and in November we filed our case with the Court of Queen's Bench.

Under Alberta law, there would not have been a problem with either of us privately adopting a child. As a couple, we would have been able to adopt a child from outside the country. But for me to adopt our son, born into our relationship, would have meant that my partner would have had to give up her maternal rights, and the role of mother would have passed from her to me. That was not what we wanted. We had to attempt to adopt under section 65(3) of the Act that states:

> *If a person adopts the child of his spouse, the child does not*
> *cease to be the child of that spouse and that spouse does not*
> *cease to be the parent and guardian of the child.*

Then there was that pesky word "spouse." We knew that we had to present any judge looking at this application with a reason to read same-sex into the word. Although not defined in the Act, "spouse" had been routinely interpreted to mean opposite-sex married, and opposite-sex common-law, couples. The application to adopt hinged on the expansion of the definition of the word "spouse" to include same-sex.

Because this case had the potential to be a Charter of Rights challenge, we had to file copies with the Federal Justice department, Alberta Child Welfare, and Alberta Justice. Our adoption hearing was scheduled for a special all-afternoon session in February 1998. In January, the Federal Justice department said that they would not interfere in the case. Child Welfare also indicated in January that they would not interfere. By the end of January, we still had not heard from the provincial Justice department, and our lawyers phoned to see what was happening. Alberta Justice claimed to have lost the paperwork, and we had to send them copies of the volumes we had already submitted to them once.

February arrived, and our excitement began to grow. Two years after first walking into the lawyers' offices, we were about to have our day in court. Then, to our dismay, the unthinkable happened. The day before our adoption hearing, the government indicated that they needed more time to assess their position on our adoption petitions, because it involved asking the Courts to make a Charter determination that "spouse" included same-sex couples. The hearing was postponed until April. It would not be the first time that we would be disappointed and tears would be shed. We had come so close!

April 2, 1998 was a day that would change the lives of gay and lesbian Albertans forever. Delwin Vriend won his case at the Supreme Court of Canada, and the Alberta government was ordered to read sexual orientation into its human rights legislation. It was a wonderful victory. Of course we had to endure a waiting game as the government debated invoking the notwithstanding clause in order not to have to follow the Supreme Court decision. It was with some relief that we applauded the Klein government's decision not to invoke the notwithstanding clause. But it was with sinking hearts that we heard pronouncement after pronouncement from Klein and various Tory cabinet ministers that, while the Vriend decision would protect homosexuals in the areas of employment, housing and access to public services, the government would not be allowing gays to be foster parents or to adopt.

Ever the optimists, we awaited our April court date, only to be frustrated once again when the government called for an adjournment so that they could take time to study the implications of the Vriend decision. Both sides met before the Chief Justice of the Court of Queen's Bench, who was appointed the case manager. The Chief Justice was responsible for ensuring that the case moved ahead in a timely manner, although he would not be hearing the case himself. He granted the government some more time, but also cautioned them against taking too much time. We waited for the decision as to whether or not the government was going to oppose our adoption bid.

The first week of September brought the most devastating news of all. The government was going to oppose our adoptions. This meant that our case now moved from the realm of adoption hearing to what is called a Trial of the Constitutional Question. This meant that we wouldn't be using our affidavits, but would actually have to bring in all the experts and the psychologist who did the home studies. They would have to be cross-examined by the government. In turn, the government would bring in its own witnesses. The trial, scheduled for April, would last about two weeks and would be extremely expensive.

We ran into a glitch when a television reporter discovered that we were going back in front of the Chief Justice in early October. When our lawyers arrived at their offices early in the morning, the parking lot was full of news trucks and cameras. To keep damage to a minimum, we hired a public-relations firm, which put out a news release stating the bare bones of the case. Soon the TV, radio, and newspapers were full of stories about our case, using terms like "ground-breaking challenge" and "likely to create a new political storm over gay rights."

Groups opposed to giving gays and lesbians equal standing in family law started making noises about the case. The president of Alberta Federation of Women United For Families (AFWUF) said that I was not a parent but "the mother's friend." She and the president of the Canada Family Action Coalition called upon the government to invoke a constitutional override, if necessary, to prevent the adoptions. One *Calgary Herald* editorial misled its readers by claiming that guardianship would provide all the benefits that adoption could, and that we did not have to re-invent traditional laws concerning marriage and what constitutes a family. The *Alberta Report* began the first of what would be monthly articles about the adoptions. The first article said that we were "homosexual activists moving forward with our agenda" and that we wanted "to suppress Alberta's Child Welfare Act." Such vitriol from people we had never met!

In the meantime, we began to raise funds. The legal bills were piling up. We began sending out hundreds of letters explaining our situation, asking for financial support as well as political support to pressure the government to allow the adoptions to go forward uncontested. The Foothills Presbytery of the United Church agreed to be an intervenor on our behalf, and we were asked to speak to several congregations about our case. One congregation, after hearing us speak, organized a letter-writing campaign the next Sunday, and 20 or 30 people came to church early in order to write letters to the government on our behalf. The generosity of complete strangers was amazing. Our fund-raising was hampered because we had to remain anonymous and our faces could not be shown due to the publication ban. We did go to court to try to get the ban lifted, but the judge, reluctant to risk the possibility, however miniscule, of some maniac trying to hurt our children if we were identified, refused to lift the ban. But money was trickling in, and every little bit helped.

January came, and the judge accepted AFWUF as intervenor for the government and the United Church as intervenors on our behalf. The trial was postponed until June, because of a complicated murder trial the judge was hearing that was taking more time than expected. We began to become experts at waiting.

On April 21, just seven weeks away from our trial, the Alberta government made an application to withdraw from the case, and Dr. Oberg advised the Legislative Assembly that the Child Welfare Act was being amended so as to allow, among other things, same-sex adoptions. The amendment changed the word "spouse" to "step-parent." Oberg openly admitted in the press that changing the law was a defensive ploy, because the government did not want the judge hearing the case to include same-sex in the interpretation of "spouse." That would have affected over 60 pieces of legislation. By changing the word to step-parent, they effectively headed off a legal and public-relations catastrophe.

By this time we had endured eleven Court appearances, five days of discovery, and the preparation and filing of three expert reports and two home assessments. We had responded to Alberta's five expert reports and hired two researchers. Our lawyers had turned over their entire practice to our case, farming out their other cases to other lawyers. Their offices were filled with stacks of boxes and binders containing all the paperwork for our case. It had become a full-time job for them.

We anxiously watched for the bill containing the amendment. It still hadn't passed the day we were scheduled to go to court to hear the government make a formal application to withdraw from the case. However, we had a letter from the government declaring the intent to pass the bill, and we had the Hansard record of Oberg's announcement. The judge accepted the government's withdrawal.

But to our dismay, to the judge's annoyance, and with no warning, AFWUF and the law firm of Fraser Milner filed a motion for "amicus curiae" or "friend of the court" status. They wanted to take up the government's case now that the government had withdrawn. This meant we had two more Court appearances, two afternoons of discovery, and the preparation of an extensive legal argument against their motion. Two weeks later, the judge rejected AFWUF's motion, and our two-week trial in June was back to a one-day adoption hearing. On May 14 the new adoption legislation passed. The word "step-parent," however, was not defined, and although we didn't believe it was problematic (after all we had the Minister on record saying it included same-sex) part of the hearing would be devoted to arguing just that point.

On June 28, 1999 we finally had our day in court. The psychologist who had done the home studies testified for most of the morning. She spoke about the literature on gay and lesbian parenting, and then spoke specifically about each of our families. In the afternoon, I went on the stand to answer questions from our lawyers about our family and my role in it. Then the other non-biological mom took the stand and spoke about her family. Presentations were made about the interpretation of "step-parent," and then it was the judge's turn.

This was an important decision, and he wanted time to carefully prepare his written decision. To our disappointment, he told us the decision would most likely come out in late July. All the lawyers felt that the judge had indicated that his decision would be a positive one. This was probably the hardest period of waiting we would have to endure.

The costs hearing took place the following week. When we first started this journey, we had no expectation of ever recouping our costs. But our lawyers argued that, due to misconduct on the government's part, we had been forced to incur costs far beyond what a "normal" step-parent adoption should cost. Legal costs were over a $100,000. It was estimated that the government had spent close to $300,000 opposing us. What a waste of money! Our lawyers also argued that because of their attempt to intervene as amicus curiae, AFWUF had forced us to incur needless extra expense, and we sought to recoup that. When the hearing was over, the judge said that he would release his decision along with the adoption decision. Then, much to our dismay, he said that he had underestimated the time he needed to write his decision and that it wouldn't be forthcoming before September. September, argghh!

I passed the summer doing my regular shifts as a volunteer at the Women's Centre and working on the Board of Directors. It was great to have somewhere to focus my energies, so that I wasn't sitting at home waiting for the lawyers to call. September passed. October passed. Most of November passed with no word. Then, on November 26, we got word that the decision was going to be released. A public-relations person was there and had already started sending out press releases and making preparations for the crowds of media people about to descend upon us.

By the time we got to the lawyers' offices, the decision had just arrived. The lawyers disappeared into an office so that they could quickly read and digest the decision. Suddenly we heard gleeful whooping, and Gary and Sam came out of their office jumping up and down in excitement. The adoptions were granted, and the government was ordered to pay our costs less the money a "normal" adoption would cost, about $2500. AFWUF was also ordered to pay costs.

We were dazed. It all seemed so unreal. Crowds of reporters filled the tiny room, camera lights blazed, and Gary and Sam made the announcement of the judge's decision in quiet voices, obviously choking back emotion. This was as exciting a moment for them as it was for us. They had been David to the government's Goliath, and they were victorious. I'm sure there were times when they despaired of ever seeing a conclusion to this case.

We did interviews for an hour or so. After the last reporter left, we cracked open the first of many bottles of champagne to be opened in the next few days. It was a quiet victory, as the publication ban is still in effect until the kids turn 18.

In April we received a new birth certificate for our son. Vital Statistics had to make up new certificates in order to accommodate the new legislation. Rather than "mother" and "father," they say "parent" and "parent." That little piece of paper is probably the most expensive birth certificate ever issued in this country. But there is now a rush to lawyers all over Alberta by lesbians and gays seeking to adopt their partners' children. We are pleased that our efforts for our families have benefited others in this province.

As for us, well you know that quiet and boring life we lead? Now that we have a government-issued piece of paper listing both of us as parents of our son, we must be a family, right? So we should be able to get Alberta Health Care benefits as a family, right? We'll have to see what the Alberta Human Rights Commission says about that. Not that we're troublemakers. We're just a quiet and boring family.

ONLY WOMEN
Anonymous

As a student I initially decided to volunteer for the Women's Centre to gain some valuable experience. When I was asked to write this excerpt I began to seriously consider why I chose to gain this experience at the Women's Centre and what has made me remain a member of this organization.

I think my choice relates to my childhood. When my parents divorced, my mother took on the responsibility of raising two children alone. Now I am 22 years old and for the past 20 years I have watched my mother successfully raise her two bi-racial children without the help of anyone else, including social assistance. As you might imagine, this was not an easy task. Not only did my mother work extremely hard to provide us with the basic necessities such as food, clothing, and a roof over our heads, but she also provided us with the proper care and support, guiding us along a healthy path. My mother instilled in both my sister and me a vital sense of worth and inner strength which has empowered us to strive for what we hope to achieve throughout life. Furthermore, my mother always encouraged us to work together.

Much of our success can be attributed to my mother, my sister, and I working as a unified team. We depend on each other for love and support, and we consider how our actions not only affect ourselves as individuals but also affect everyone in our family. For instance, I remember the time my sister and I were almost kicked out of daycare due to our disobedient behaviour. Realizing how much our mother depended on childcare to supervise us while she worked provided enough encouragement for us to quickly change our ways. I realize that most families probably work as a team, but with the absence of one parent, the members of a single parent family feel the need to depend on each other so much more.

You may be wondering exactly how this relates to the Women's Centre. Being raised in a house of only women may be why I feel more comfortable in a centre of only women, but my reasons for joining the Centre are more significant than this. Overall, the Women's Centre teaches and reinforces the same lessons I was taught throughout childhood. Their resources, services, and workshops empower women so they too can achieve their goals and strive for a better quality of life. Members unite and work together to reach these goals. I of course advocate the Women's Centre as these lessons have led me to become the strong, independent woman I am today.

THE WRC AT THE YWCA
Sandi Carlisle

A desk, a chair, a City of Calgary AID (Advice Information and Direction) directory, old files from the Status of Women Action Committee, a part-time co-ordinator, and a lounge at the YWCA launched the resurrected Women's Resource Centre in May, 1979. It was a second beginning in the history of a place just for women.

From the end of 1973 to the end of 1976, the YWCA operated a Women's Resource Centre with a part-time co-ordinator. The Centre was forced to close due to uncertain funding, sporadic operating hours, and the emergence of the Calgary Status of Women Action Committee as a source of information.

With the support of a new Executive Director, Maureen Crane, a movement began in 1978 to reopen the Centre. Board members recognized the importance of providing a central place for women seeking information, support, and direction in order to fully realize their potential. Funding for the Centre was included in the YWCA's five-year plan with the recognition that paid staff would be crucial to the stability of the Centre. Calgary SWAC turned over their information and professional resource files to the YWCA as their focus changed to political action and the publishing of the *Calgary Women's Newspaper*.

Recognizing their need for community support and seeking community input, the YWCA invited representatives of community agencies primarily serving women to a luncheon. Lively discussion and enthusiastic response confirmed the need for a women's resource centre and on May 1, 1979 the Centre was born.

News spread very quickly, mostly by word of mouth, about

the comfortable place where women could meet, exchange ideas and tell their stories, as well as find help, advocacy, and referrals for specific needs. A place where women help women—a place to begin.

In response to the needs expressed by women in the Calgary community, a variety of groups and services were initiated: a weekly free legal advice clinic staffed by lawyers and law students in co-operation with Calgary Legal Guidance; a Women for Sobriety group; discussion groups; a job search support group; a networking group called the Calgary Women's Network; and peer counseling.

Volunteers played the most important role in the functioning of the Centre, then as now. Students from the faculty of Social Work at the University of Calgary and from Mount Royal College found their practicum placements at the Women's Resource Centre a valuable place for applying theories learned in classes.

At the end of my four years as co-ordinator, up to 1200 women per month were using the many services of the YWCA's Women's Resource Centre. Today, 21 years later, the Women's Centre as an independent service is still a vital, thriving, and necessary part of the Calgary community.

THE IMPORTANCE OF BEING HYSTERICAL

Jane Cawthorne

I know I am often hysterical or on the edge of hysteria. I feel the day to day, not-enough-hours-in-the-day kind of hysteria that comes with being a woman, a wife, a mother, a mother who also works outside the home, a daughter, and a caregiver to many people, family and non-family. There are hysterical moments when the dishwasher is full, the phone is ringing, and the TV is too loud, and I notice out of the corner of my eye that my daughter has changed the channel to something that looks like it might be *Basic Instinct*, and the doorbell rings, and a pile of unopened mail is about to slide off the edge of the kitchen counter; and I still don't know what to have for dinner.

I feel hysteria when my young daughter utters some newly-discovered, objectionable word or mimics some small trait that shows the callousness of the world outside our home. I stare in disbelief and work quickly through my initial hysterical reaction to deliver a calm and measured speech about the importance of being respectful to others and about how behaving respectfully differs from what-ever I just witnessed. These are hysterical moments in which I know I need to do some teaching and quickly get on with the job.

I feel hysteria when I realize someone I love is sick, very sick, and I can do nothing to help. I come face to face with mortality. This is the hysteria of grief and mourning, mixed with anger, frustration, and sadness.

I feel hysteria when I read the newspaper. I sometimes weep when I read about famine, about homelessness, about pain of all sorts. People argue over whether or not the tapes of two brutal

murders of two mothers' daughters should be open for public view-
ing. Who would want to see them? What kind of person would etch
those images into their brain? I throw the paper into the recycling
bin, check back to ensure that it's face down, and move on.

But there is another kind of hysteria. It is buried much deeper.
Calm on the outside, I feel hysteria at leaving my child behind in
order to participate in the big world beyond my small family. I must
separate my role as a mother from my role in everything else I do in
the world, as though mothering exists separately.

I feel hysteria when I am faced with the vestiges of patriarchal
power, "old boys" who patronize me. I remember, as a young
teacher, being asked by a male colleague when I would leave teaching and have children. When did society ever ask men to choose
between being fathers or workers, men or citizens?

Most disturbing of all is the hysteria I feel when I recognize the
disparity between what I expect to be like in the world and what I
am like in the world. I claim to be an environmentalist, but I drive a
car. I am sometimes too lazy to compost. I claim to care about social
justice, but I have material possessions well beyond what I need. I
know that my comfort is directly related to the discomfort of others,
my morning coffee the ingestion of another person's exploitation on
a plantation somewhere in Colombia or Mexico or Guatemala. I do
what I can and work within the realm of my knowledge, experience,
and expertise to use my privilege as a platform from which to speak,
to advocate for change, and to create conditions in which social
inequity will be reduced. The first of the twelve steps is recognizing
that you have a problem. I fight my discomfort and try to move
ahead as part of the solution. I try to teach my child to do the same.

Phrases like "social justice" and "the common good" have almost
disappeared from our collective vocabulary. I feel hysteria rise when
I talk about these ideas and I am dismissed. I hear comments about
balanced budgets and the importance of reducing deficits and I am

exasperated. It is not that I cannot support fiscal responsibility—that is a given. But why is it that social spending is continually sacrificed while subsidies for corporate interests continue unabated? What about the legacy we pass on in crumbling infrastructure, in poor health care, by under-investing in education, in failing to find ways to equitably distribute the world's food, in failing to address global climate change? Can the brokers of the status quo create even a small space to admit that these are actual problems, let alone have the tenacity to try to solve them? I am hysterical at the smugness of these people. I am hysterical that because of their refusal to admit there is a problem, solutions suggested by people much smarter than me will never be implemented. The power brokers in our society have too much to lose. Weibo Ludwig is found guilty. But the polluters are free to continue with their business. This is incomplete justice.

Hysteria. My handy pocket Oxford defines it as a wild, uncontrollable emotion or excitement or a functional disturbance of the nervous system of psychoneurotic origin. Root word: hystera, from which we also get hysterectomy, which is of course the surgical removal of the uterus. Hysteria is typically considered a bad thing, a woman's thing, a thing to be removed.

Only women are described as hysterical, and this description is usually applied to a woman who is railing against some established norm. You may have heard her described as strident, as a feminist, as a radical. In Alberta, she is often called a "left-wing nut" by government types. If only she could recognize the folly of her thinking and join the common sense revolution, or whatever they are calling defending the status quo this week. If only she were more like a man. What makes us different from men, our women's bodies or our work of care-giving in our society, is the source of some kind of craziness, abnormality, difference, otherness. It makes us hysterical. Remove it, and we will once again be rational, normal, or the same as men. But for me, hysteria manifests itself when what I know is

61

necessary to nurture and sustain life is silenced, ignored, absent, or ripped away from me.

I do not dismiss hysteria as an outmoded stereotype applied to women, or deny that it actually happens or that it is a real state that women get into. I embrace hysteria. I recognize it as a wise friend. I have learned to welcome its arrival and learn from its presence. Hysteria, in the immortal words of Martha Stewart, is a "good thing." It is a sign to myself that something is not right. It is a disruption of the comfort zone, a fact of my life that makes it impossible for me to sit back and do nothing.

SOMEONE TO TALK TO
Anonymous

I found the Women's Centre one day when I was feeling lonely. I had just left a bad marriage and had no friends to talk to. I saw the Women's Centre sign near the Safeway on 10th Street, and I thought I would see if they could help me. Ivon was there. She talked to me and suggested that I sign up for Spanish classes—to get me out of the house and give me a chance to meet other women.

I don't remember much of the Spanish I learned, but it was a big help to go to the Centre and spend time with other women. I gradually got involved in other things: I joined the quilting group, I fought back when the Centre was about to be closed down, and I went on the International Women's Day March. What a great feeling that was!

Now I volunteer on the phones at the Centre one day a week and I help women find all the services they need. It feels good to know that I'm helping other women who are feeling the way I felt that day eight years ago when I needed someone to talk to.

About four years ago, I started tutoring an elderly Chinese-speaking woman in English. We met once a week, one on one. I helped her with her English and she brought me lunch. She even came to my home and made me Thanksgiving dinner. I have MS and can't cook. I felt very much like Hau was my second mother, and I really loved going to the Centre to teach her English. We helped each other.

When my Dad had a heart attack, he was far away and there was nothing I could do for him. I was upset and scared. It was important to have good friends to talk to; they helped me get through it all.

I've had a lot of fun and good times at the Women's Centre. So many laughs and great pot-luck parties. I even met my husband there. One of the other volunteers brought him in, and we noticed each other right away. He made a joke about not being married because he couldn't find a woman who "knew her place." Boy, was that the wrong thing to say! I called him up and told him that maybe he should have coffee with me so I could straighten him out about wanting a doormat for a wife. Of course, he didn't mean what he had said and we hit it off right away. We got married a year ago in Grande Prairie and women from the Centre drove up for the wedding.

The Women's Centre feels like a family to me, and I wouldn't miss my day of answering the phones for anything. Even when my MS flares up, I know I can still help out—if I can't manage the phones, there is always something I can do. My life is much better because of the Women's Centre.

Highbush Cranberry: Northern Survival
Carole Thorpe

How to tell your story, a woman's story. Walking into the Women's Centre in Bridgeland, Calgary. A traveller armed with Her Story: a Daytimer, dictionary, thumb sketches, sketchbooks, photographs, and poetry. Stories of my mother and grandmothers breathing over my shoulders. Herstory: images of women from photographs, paintings, oral history. How my story begins to be reshaped when I interact with the women who walk into the Women's Centre. Back out into the streets. Back out into the patriarchal culture that wounds us through our mixed-up relationships with men. And with each other. How do I bring my story into collaboration with other women's stories? So that communication becomes open, constructive, educational, and healing? How to tell a story with the grace of my ancestral voices, with female muses, goddesses, and myths guiding me?

I live a few blocks away from The Women's Centre in a small house that I've lived in since 1986. I now live in the house alone, because in September 1999 I separated from my husband after 17 years. I am going through difficult changes as I try to thread my way through the relics of that relationship. What to preserve, what to throw away? In the autumn of 1999 I participated in the Women's Safety Program, sponsored by the Women's Centre, the Calgary Women's Immigration Association, and several other organizations. The program coincided with my separation and it was an excellent source of information.

As I struggle to survive through this period, I am gaining insights into women's issues on many fronts. I have been studying yoga for about seven years and this helps me to try to balance mind, body, and spirit. Easier said than done. Anxieties and fears pile in and I often feel overwhelmed. The Women's Centre has become a haven for me, particularly at this time. My old support systems are disappearing. I have deleted family functions with in-laws from my Daytimer: New Year's, Easter, Thanksgiving, Christmas, birthdays, barbeques. This is the context for my story in the present.

I was born in 1954 and raised in Montreal, Quebec. I am fortunate to have received an abundance of stories from my family. Stories from my mother, Cecelia Anne Roy Thorpe, and my grandmother, Georgina Simpson Ross Roy, have shaped my creative work. I work as a visual artist, writer, and glassblower. In 1983, I graduated in printmaking from the Alberta College of Art. In 1998, I graduated with a BA in English from the University of Calgary.

Since 1986, I have learned glassblowing from my husband and business partner. I am co-owner of a glass business where I make production items: bowls, perfume bottles, vases, paperweights, and jewelry. As I struggle through the process of separation and divorce, my relationship to several communities and to my in-laws is changing. As I write this, I've survived nine months since September 1999—my gestation period for my new life. Everything is still being negotiated—marital property and the glass business. This process feels like plate tectonics; large chunks of my life are shifting and I don't know how they will be rearranged.

There are some days when I feel incapable of tackling these problems. On days when I'm tired and depressed, I sometimes struggle with migraine headaches and allergies. My training in yoga often revives me as I focus on breathing, stretching, endurance, and spirituality. On days when I am stronger and more energetic, my single life brings unexpected surprises. I am free to meet new people and engage in politics that reflect my beliefs. I can continue my education and creative work without the marital conflicts that sometimes prevented me from pursuing projects. Sometimes, living alone gives me the freedom to work and play on my own terms; other times, I am plagued by loneliness and insecurity.

Within the next year, I hope to continue the projects that I have already started. I also want to focus on new creative work. Some projects will be designed to bring in money; other projects will be experimental and less likely to bring in money. I have a "mixed career" portfolio of work that I need to re-evaluate and re-define. My past visual arts work includes printmaking, painting, drawing, constructions, and installations in various Canadian galleries. Most of my income has been derived from my glass business; glass pieces have been marketed in several commercial Canadian galleries and other outlets. I've had poetry, short stories, and creative documentary pieces (a genre that combines creativity with personal narratives) published in several Canadian literary magazines.

I will probably let go of more things as my divorce is settled. Although some of these changes are traumatic and exhausting, I am trying to prepare myself for career changes. The symbol that I some-times use to represent writing, art, glass, and interdisciplinary projects is Vibernum. I'm interested in the native shrub, highbush cranberry (*Viburnum trilobum*), which is more closely related to honeysuckle than the true cranberry bush. Highbush cranberry, which survives and adapts in the northern Canadian environment, is also an edible fruit and traditional medicine. I often use the maple-shaped leaves and red berries for ceremonies. Vibernum empowers me in my personal life and work.

A New Friend
Nickie Surveyer

Even though my time with the Women's Centre has been brief, I feel that I have a sense of its history through the people who make up the heart of the Centre. That would be the people who access it, staff, and volunteers. Each of these women has a story to tell. My story is about a day or two or three in the life of the Centre. Well, in this case, it is a Thursday morning. I start the day off with a cup of the co-ordinator's coffee, and if that doesn't give me a jump-start, nothing will. Wait a minute—I am getting ahead of myself here. Let me go back to the beginning.

Discovering the Women's Centre has been like making a new friend. Instead of one person, it's a place full of people to learn with and share experiences with. The Women's Centre became a part of my life because of my need for support and my desire to help others within the community. In the middle of a career transition, I found the resources and people at the Centre to be a welcome respite from feeling disconnected at times.

My acquaintance with the Centre began last year. I came in looking for information about the Women's Centre and I had many questions about accessing the Internet. What I found was a place full of colourful masks, quilts, and generous people. The volunteer co-ordinator took the time to meet with me and patiently explained how to access the Internet. I found everyone easy to talk to and exchange ideas with. So I left feeling that I had stumbled across a wonderfully comfortable place to do some research and meet new people. It felt good knowing that the Centre was there for me. Having the Women's Centre in my neighbourhood was an added bonus!

The rest is history. I am happy to say that I became a volunteer with the Women's Centre approximately a year ago. The Centre has provided me with the opportunity to offer my skills and learn new skills while helping people.

An important characteristic of the Women's Centre is the feeling of welcome extended by staff, volunteers, and the people who access the Centre. It is a feeling of connection. Being able to share in a discussion over a cup of coffee, or just sit down and review some pamphlets, or borrow a book, or work on the computer. I feel that whatever has brought someone to the Women's Centre is why it is there.

A typical day for me has included helping a group of women practice their English while sharing friendship, stories, and laughter. For me it was an amazing experience; I immediately felt welcome and part of a collaborative learning process. I could not resist the temptation of selecting an article that covered the different varieties of chocolate. Just for fun of course. Can you blame me?

Maybe the term "typical day" does not apply to the Women's Centre, because I have found that there is no such thing. As a peer support volunteer, I answer the phone and do a variety of things as they occur. The mornings can simply whiz by and they can also move at an easy pace: it really depends. This is what makes it fun and interesting.

My primary role as a peer support volunteer is to provide support and information to people who call or drop by. I am consistently in awe of the strength of the women and families who share their stories while searching for information and assistance. These experiences have taught me how much we have to learn from one another.

I feel that listening is the most important part of being a volunteer with the Centre. I hope that, in doing so, I have been able to provide some assistance while extending an invitation to the women and families to explore the Centre further.

There you have it. I hope that my story has successfully captured some of the qualities and experiences that make up the Women's Centre. It is not always easy to convey your thoughts and feelings accurately when putting pen to paper. But it was important to me to make the attempt. In closing, I would like to say that it has been, and continues to be, a pleasure being a part of the Women's Centre. Thank you for being there.

My 60 Years of Being a Woman
Anonymous

My mother nearly died trying to abort me, using home-made instruments with no medical supervision. Both my parents relayed this story, in various gory versions, over and over to me for as long as I can remember. It did not take long before I understood that I was indeed a terrible person. I don't remember my mother ever hugging me, let alone saying she loved me.

My father is an alcoholic and my mother is addicted to prescription drugs. My first sexual encounter was with my drunken father at the age of eight. I was beaten up both physically and verbally for years. My older sister escaped most of this because she learned to never question, ask for anything or speak unless spoken to. I was quite different and spoke out far too much, disobeyed often, and was generally rebellious. From the age of eight, aside from the time I was in school, I was responsible for my newborn sister, for cooking meals, and for cleaning a nine-room house.

We lived in a small city, and I had some wonderful times during my teen years. I was quite popular as well as pretty, so my mother liked to show me off. I was allowed to take figure skating lessons. I had lovely clothes. I was involved in a little theatre, took ballet, and was a cheerleader for school events as well as for our city hockey team. Although I had much to do at home and a sister to care for, my life outside the house was wonderful. I learned to be very fast and efficient around the house. I was a good cook (and I enjoyed cooking), but I was most unkind to my little sister. I left her unattended far too often and treated her badly. I didn't like her at all and

I remember being down right mean to her on many occasions. To this day, I try not to think about those times as I feel so bad.

When I was 15, I met a fellow who was on the same bowling team as I was. He was nine years my senior and knew both my parents well. He turned out to be my Prince Charming. I started dating him and we married when I was 18. I became pregnant immediately and, oddly enough, my mother discovered she was having a surprise baby. My sister was born in March and my daughter in September.

My husband and I were very poor, but I was content. He dearly loved me and I cannot tell anyone how wonderful it is to have someone love you just the way you are. We moved to a large city, and the only time things were terrible was when we went home to visit. My husband and our son stayed with his folks while my daughter and I stayed with my parents. My father blew a hole through our living room wall with a shotgun and threatened to kill us all in one of his drunken rages. My mother overdosed on sleeping pills and nearly died. My father threw me across the room on more than one occasion.

My husband and I moved to yet another city where we both worked two jobs to try to get ahead. I babysat children in our home and worked at a drugstore at night while my husband drove a cab. During this time my mother had two affairs that I knew of. She finally left my father and my youngest sister (aged six at the time) for another man. My father did not cope well at all as I soon realized when he and my little sister came for what was to be a short visit. He was deeply depressed to the point where I had to have him hospitalized due to a complete mental breakdown. He was in treatment for six weeks during which time I cared for my youngest sister. She was in constant trouble—lying, stealing, and causing problems—and I had to have the police to our home because of neighbour complaints. Another younger sister attempted suicide. My older sister divorced and remarried a fellow who committed suicide. So all in all, this was a very difficult time.

After four years in that city, we made our last move—to Calgary. I was pregnant with our third child, which absolutely delighted both my husband and myself. I went to work when our little girl was three months old, and I consider this to be a very busy but happy time in my life. My world was shaken to its foundation when my husband was diagnosed with terminal cancer. I was 36. The next ten years were difficult—I worked full time, had our children to tend and a husband I visited each and every day. After he died, I went to school at nights to upgrade and became a workaholic. Within five years of my husband's death, my son was diagnosed with Multiple Sclerosis and my youngest sister (aged 30) committed suicide. During the next five years my youngest sister's son also committed suicide. But life goes on.

After my husband died, my life was almost unbearable. How did I survive? By reaching out. I had one dear friend who sat up many nights with me just listening. I went to Women's Retreats where I was counseled on journal writing and meditating. I joined support groups where I held others up and they held me up. I turned to my church where I was welcomed with open arms and given much spiritual support. I joined some fun groups—walking, hiking, theatre, and golf. I joined a palliative care team where I shared my story and gained much strength. I took in many personal growth seminars and gained a sense of worthiness and purpose. I sought medical help; I have had counseling more than once. I threw myself into my job where I worked far too many hours but loved it. I worked on a very large staff with wonderful people. I adopted them all and they became like family to me.

Where am I now? What does all this say? It says that I have discovered there are many resources available to us if we only reach out. I retired last year and had a very difficult and lonely time. Once again, I reached out and learned how wonderful life can be. I have had many, many wonderful friends. I have earned a living. I have kind and beautiful children and grandchildren I adore and enjoy more than I can ever say. I have learned that I will only be as happy as I allow myself to be. I have learned to forgive my parents and go forward—to adopt some dear friends as my family and not be afraid to ask for emotional help. "It's not the road we have walked that matters, it's what we do on the path ahead that counts."

I often say a that a good friend is like a favourite book. The longer you have them, the more you treasure them. Self-esteem and a sense of inner happiness are things I will have to keep working on forever. Life is not without pain, sorrow, or disappointment for all of us. It is a challenge but one well worth taking. With the help of the resources I have mentioned plus many others that are available, the journey can be an adventure of self-discovery and contentment. Yes, life is good.

Friendship and Support: The Practice English Group

Rita Gin

I go to the Women's Centre every Tuesday for English class. The very first time I came here, I already noticed that the staff here is very nice, friendly, easy to approach, and eager to answer questions. The atmosphere here is very homey; you feel comfortable once you come in. Besides the English class here every Tuesday, the Women's Centre has classes for cooking and crafts on other days. There are a lot of free consulting services here too.

I find it a blessing to have a place such as the Women's Centre here in Calgary, where women can make genuine friends, advise each other about daily life, and take courses.

Angela Lee

I came to the Women's Centre about half a year ago. The reason for my coming is because I have to accompany a lady who needs to be involved in community activities.

Phung is the lady I have to accompany. We like the Women's Centre very much. First of all, we like the drive to this Centre. It is nice to drive along the beautiful banks of the Bow River to get here.

The ladies in the Women's Centre are very nice and friendly. We get together to learn to speak English and how to write English. As we learn English we get to know each other and sometimes we can laugh at each other's jokes.

In this Centre we can meet ladies of different backgrounds. Most of the ladies come from Hong Kong and one lady came from Korea. Some ladies are married and have children or grandchildren. I am surprised to find out that there is one single lady and one child-less lady. They are very brave to live in Calgary all by themselves. I guess this Centre provides a lot of support and encouragement for them.

In the future I hope this Centre will help and support a lot of women, not only Asian descendants, but a lot more of other ethnic groups. All of them can find this Women's Centre as their second home, a place where they can find trust, understanding, friendship, and support.

Daisy Yau

I need to learn English. So I looked in the Chinese newspaper. I found out there is a Women's Centre, and that the Women's Centre is very close to my home.

Coming to the Women's Centre improved my English. It is to make more women friends of my age. And they give me experience for my life. I don't like cooking, but I am very interested to learn to cook. So I love the Women's Centre very much.

Hye-Kyung Cho

I went to the Women's Centre last October. My friend Stella came with me to the Women's Centre. Before, I didn't know about the Women's Centre project. Now, I understand the Women's Centre project. What does the Women's Centre do? At the Women's Centre we meet new friends, learn to cook another country's food, study

English, and learn new skills.

These are some women's problems: childcare, child support, child custody, education, legal problems. Women's Centre settles women's problems.

Every Tuesday I come to study English.

I am very happy.

Stella Chao

I am so lucky that I have a chance to study in the Women's Centre since September 1999. It is a great association to assist our women, especially the immigrant women. In there, the staff and teachers are so nice and friendly to us. I learn English and make friends with my classmates.

There are also many other subjects for us to learn, such as cooking, quilting, knitting, etc. Sometimes, they also arrange for us to attend some outside activities.

Women's Centre is a very good place. I enjoy being there.

MORE TO GIVE
Jill Martland

I have been privileged to have the choice to be a stay-at-home mother. My story begins 18 years ago, when I had four small children, a good marriage, and financial stability. My life was frantic; I was always rushing to drive carpools, getting the kids to programs, and volunteering for all their schools (four at one point). I was involved in an education committee, parent council, and other activities— soccer, hockey, Brownies, and Beavers. And I spent up to forty hours a week running the Calgary Folk Club & Festival where my husband played with the host band. I was also running a campaign to designate our local elementary school as bilingual, and I remember spending up to six hours a day on the phone. I spent every afternoon helping to teach computers at our local elementary. Our house was the liveliest on the block—I took a couple of extras for lunch, encouraged my kids to have their friends over, and considered the neighbours' kids family, as they spent most of their free time with us. I would often feel sick in the morning, wondering how I would get through the day, and not have the time or energy for my kids. My husband worked long hours and was usually only home for an hour at dinner before returning to work. I was regularly up until 2:00 AM, trying to get accounts, grant applications, budgets, and reports for the Folk Club done while it was quiet. Meanwhile, I wondered why my life seemed so difficult as I was "just a housewife." What was wrong with me that I couldn't handle it all? Why wasn't I happy? I had so much to be grateful for with a wonderful family, my health, and all I wanted.

It was at this stage that I became ill with a tumor, followed by surgery and convalescence. My body was telling me that I needed to make some changes. I signed up for an evening course called *Contemporary Woman* and learned that I had needs too and that I had given everything to my family at the expense of meeting these needs. The analogy was with a pitcher: the more you fill it, the more you have to give. I was running on empty. I learned to refuse some of the requests for baking, canvassing, helping in the schools, looking after friends' kids, and so forth. I unloaded much of the work I was doing and scheduled time for walks, friends, baths, and reading. I also began to look at what I would really enjoy in the way of volunteer work, and that led me to the Women's Resource Centre at the YWCA, currently the Women's Centre.

Eighteen years later, the Women's Centre is still an important part of my life. Besides sitting on the Board and doing fund-raising, the most rewarding part for me is the direct service. The Centre keeps me in touch with what is going on for women in Calgary, and I enjoy my interaction with clients through peer counseling and through staffing the desk. Another important aspect is the friendships with the staff and the other volunteers, and the social get-togethers with so many wonderful women. The Centre exposes me to women from all walks of life and all segments of society, women who teach me much and enrich my life in many ways. If I go into work feeling that I have problems, things are put into perspective in a hurry.

Over the years, the work and clients have changed significantly, and the Centre has managed to shift its focus to accommodate the changing times. When I began, fewer of the clients were women living in poverty. More were concerned with transition in their lives: leaving relationships, dealing with being left, returning to the work force, learning to value themselves, and becoming feminists. Women were learning to speak out on abuse and social issues. Many women were dealing with low self-esteem and lack of assertiveness and were beginning to learn that they could wield power. Groups were forming to allow women to support one another through many of these transitions and in their social action. Women were finding their strength and seeking help to do so through counseling and through the support of other women.

With the erosion of government services over the years and cutbacks in all areas, the Centre now deals mainly with clients living in poverty. Many agencies have shut their doors, and we aim to cover these gaps in services. More of our clients are in crisis, and we help in any way we can. We will never know the extent of our role in preventive services, but I am sure it is significant.

Women's Centre, long may we thrive!

GETTING MONEY
Lucette Simpson and *Anne Spicer*

When things go wrong, as they sometimes will,
When the road you're trudging seems all uphill,
When the funds are low and the debts are high,
And you want to smile, but you have to sigh,
When care is pressing you down a bit,
Rest, if you must—but don't you quit.

The author of this verse is unknown, but in the fall of 1994, she might have penned it after walking into the YWCA Women's Resource Centre on 10th Street NW. Instead of being greeted by the familiar, warm glow of enthusiasm, she would have found Centre staff and volunteers lost in gloomy contemplation. Word had just been received that the Centre would be shut down because anticipated funding was not available.

At this time, the funding in question was $33,000—a paltry sum. Surely, if everyone pulled together and came up with good fund-raising ideas, we could easily obtain this money and more. We couldn't just quit.

Ah, the shining visions of neophytes! It wasn't long before we understood that the Centre's needs were not this simple. By then, however, the fires had been struck and we were determined to achieve our fund-raising goals. After careful research and review, we decided that the Centre needed an Endowment Fund of $500,000 to meet its operational needs, maintain and initiate good programs, and reduce its dependency on outside funding. We saw no reason why we couldn't attain this goal within five years and we set about to make it happen.

Fresh from our initial fund-raising event—a raffle that yielded $1,000—the newly formed fund-raising committee steadied its sea legs and began to brainstorm other fund-raising possibilities. We were excited, full of purpose, and extremely naïve. When the YWCA gave us the green light to set up the Endowment fund, they did not inform us about the restrictions that would apply. We could not hold a golf tournament because the YWCA was contemplating doing the same. Nor could we approach certain corporations because of the YWCA's capital campaign. Confusion and frustration soon replaced our new-found optimism.

But the committee was determined and continued to encourage people to donate to our fund. In June 1997 the YWCA gave us the go-ahead to hold a golf tournament—our first major fund-raising effort. With positive feedback from sponsors and from players, we decided that this would become an annual event. Feeling that we had managed to overcome most of the hurdles that had held up our fund-raising efforts, we were pleased to have raised $21,000 for the Endowment Fund by the fall of 1997.

Shortly thereafter, we received devastating news. The YWCA decided to put its efforts into new endeavours. The Women's Resource Centre would be reduced to a magazine rack in the YWCA lobby, offering brochures about agencies that could be of assistance to women. This announcement elicited a quick response from volunteers and friends of the Centre. Through their efforts, the Centre reopened under a new name and without the protective umbrella of the YWCA. The Women's Centre was born. An alliance with Oxfam-Canada allowed us to continue to raise funds under their charitable status until the Centre could obtain its own charitable status. In the neat and tidy world of fund-raising, building partnerships with sponsors and setting up long-lasting programs require time. The Centre's independence, however, changed the course of our fund-raising. We abandoned long-range planning in favour of quickly finding money to keep the Centre alive.

With this greater urgency, we had to accelerate our efforts. We organized yet another golf tournament and we raised money by volunteering at casinos and at Stampeder football games. We started a "Shrinking Coffee Party" because this event had the potential to raise $136,000. The idea was to invite seven women to a coffee party, asking each to donate $10. They, in turn, would each have a coffee party with six guests and these guests would also donate $10. This would continue until a coffee party of one person was held. This idea created a lot of awareness for the Women's Centre, but only raised $9,500. We still felt that the idea had promise and decided to hold a different type of coffee party.

Why coffee parties? We are an organization that helps women to help themselves. Part of helping each other is getting to know one another. The best way to get to know one another is chatting over a hot cup of coffee. Look at the surge of new coffee establishments in this city to understand the appeal. We decided to call our new event "Coffee Connections." For one day each year, we invite people to host a coffee party and ask their guests to donate to the Women's Centre. We feel that this is a successful approach to raising funds and we plan to expand this event.

We have introduced another fund-raising tool that makes it easy for everyone to support the Women's Centre: our Monthly Contribution Plan. Donors commit to giving monthly sums that fit into their budgets, as little as $5 per month. The donor's bank account is debited on the first of each month and a tax receipt is issued in the early part of the following year.

We took a break from hosting the golf tournament this year to review past efforts and to prepare for the future. The golf tournament is highly popular and an attractive venue for the right sponsors. We are actively searching for sponsor support.

The Women's Centre is funded in part by the United Way and

by the City of Calgary. The rest of our operating funds, approximately $60,000 annually, we must raise ourselves.

We are fortunate to have many volunteers who selflessly give a great deal of their time to our events. Calgary is well known for the generosity of its citizens and for the many fund-raising initiatives undertaken by a myriad of groups. Despite the largesse of Calgarians, we find it more and more difficult to compete for funds, especially since we are a small and relatively unknown agency. We are searching for more sponsor support in order to become better known throughout the community, to ease our current requirements, and to allow us to once again build long-range funding solutions. The Women's Centre has a place in this city and its importance is increasing with our rapidly growing population.

Fund-raising takes patience, initiative, and the help of many. We've fought and won battles over the past few years and we are ready to face the challenges we will need to meet in order to reach self-sufficiency. If the wag who penned the words that opened this article were to add another verse, it might read something like this:

> *It's up to each man what becomes of him;*
> *He must find in himself the grit and vim*
> *That brings success; he can get the skill*
> *If he brings to the task a steadfast will.*

REFLECTIONS
Almas Rajwani-Rawji

In every woman's life, there comes a time when she sits down and reflects on the women who have touched her life in many, many different ways. Some women we never forget—like our mothers or our grandmothers. With others, it is the things they teach us that we never forget. This is the story of one woman who left me with a great experience in patience.

It was a warm Saturday morning in spring. The tulips were budding in almost every garden—red, pink, and yellow. They were everywhere. There was a fresh smell of earth, grass, and lilacs. Life could go on forever, I thought to myself.

I rang the doorbell of #88 and a gentleman answered the door. I introduced myself as the palliative care volunteer he had requested and he welcomed me warmly with a bright smile. He walked me to his wife's bedroom and introduced me in turn. A very slim, pale, and pretty woman in blue turned to look at me and then looked away again. She looked angry and anxious and stated that she did not want me in her room. Her husband had to go to work for the whole day, and he needed me to stay there, no matter what.

I was asked to sit in the family room and could only go in the patient's room to serve her lunch. That was fine. Thank goodness for books and magazines, I thought to myself. As I sat there, I began to realize that this volunteering position was a lesson in patience for me. I had had very little patience in the past. At 6:00 PM the husband returned and I left. On Sunday, I again rang the doorbell at 9:00 AM. I sat in the family room, except to serve lunch, and left at 6:00 PM.

The next weekend was different. When I went to say hello to my patient, she turned to look at me and invited me to sit in her room and watch TV with her. I was so happy. This was my first assignment and I wanted to be a good palliative care volunteer. The day was meaningful for me and for "Sammy." We talked a little. I gave her a back rub because her back was sore from lying down. I helped her change and managed to get her to come into the kitchen to have her lunch. After lunch, she suggested that we sit outside on the patio. She had not done this for a long time, and she missed it. While "Sammy" rested, I decided to prepare supper so that her husband would come home to dinner. This time when I left at 6:00 PM, my patient and I had a cheery goodbye. I was one happy volunteer. I knew that if my patient had her rough days, it would be a lesson in patience for me.

And so I spent my weekends with "Sammy" and did I ever learn to enjoy her. I met the rest of the family: her two daughters who hardly came to visit because they were not happy to learn that mom was "full of cancer." I also met her youngest child, 17-year-old Peter, who went off to sleep at a friend's now and then because "Mom is too sick to take care of me anymore." Every lunch hour on the weekends, we had a hungry visitor and did it ever cheer my patient. Her son loved the warm, appetizing sandwiches that I prepared for him and she got to see her son more regularly. He even started to come by during the weekdays. I learned a lot from my patient, and we both knew that her time was drawing to an end. I dreaded that moment, but when I saw how much pain she suffered, I could not help but pray that she would be relieved of it sooner rather than later.

When I was told that "Sammy" was in a coma, I burst into tears. This was the one thing I had dreaded the most: I would not have the opportunity to speak with her before her final time. I almost ran through the corridors of the hospital and let my tears flow as I stood by her bed. I visited every day, hoping that I would be able to speak to her one more time—to thank her for letting me volunteer with her and to thank her for the lessons she taught me about people who need more patience. At one point I went to the minister and asked him to pray with me, and he said a beautiful prayer for her. The next day she passed away. She was my first patient in palliative care volunteering, but not my last, and I will never forget the experience she left me with.

I hope wherever she is, she is in peace.

LISTENING
Agnieszka Wolska Chaney

I decided to spend my time volunteering for the Women's Centre because I have been surrounded by women all my life. My family happened to be made up mainly of women, while the few men (including my dad) of the family seemed to be on the outside of where "my" women gathered—my grandma's kitchen. My mom, two sisters, three cousins, three aunts, my grandma, and my great grandma cooking and talking and making hand-made pasta or pastries on a Sunday afternoon...I learned so much from them throughout my childhood. Even when I rebelled against learning to cook or cleaning a chicken, I learned so much more than the lessons seemed to teach me.

Perhaps this is why I decided that I wanted to help women. Perhaps it was my anger at the disrespect and discrimination that these amazing women in my family experience continually back in rural Poland and my anger at the abuse and violence women experience everywhere in the world.

When I started volunteering at the Women's Centre, shortly before I started my Social Work training in the fall of 1999, I was afraid to face clients whose stories were painful. I would quickly pass the phone onto someone more experienced. After a while, I realized that there is no need to run from my discomfort or hide behind a lack of knowledge. I realized that as women, we share many similar experiences—not the same, by any means, but similar. And we care and cry and laugh in similar ways. Helping other women is not about having more knowledge. It is about listening to my soul. I am very young still and have little knowledge or experience, but I care, and I learned here at the Women's Centre that this is all that counts.

INTERVIEW WITH THE CO-CHAIR
Natalie Simpson with Nora Stewart

— *When did you become involved with the Women's Centre and why?*
I became involved with the Women's Centre in 1997, when the program was shut down at the YWCA, and they started looking for another place to open the Centre. I knew Yvonne Stanford (another board member) who told me about the place. I felt that the services that the Women's Centre had been providing were important to carry on.

I participated in the coffee party once two years ago and when I came on the board I also volunteered at the football games, but up until then I hadn't done any volunteering. Any charity work that I had been involved with before was fund-raising for schools. So this is my first step into a major role in a charitable organization.

—*Do you consider yourself to be a feminist?*
Yes. I think I align myself with women who call themselves feminists. I'm comfortable with the term, although I know some people have problems with the term. I have a hard time articulating why some people connect feminism with radical behaviour. It is becoming more comfortable for me to be labeled as someone with radical behaviour. I don't know that I am that radical, but if people want to call me that I am comfortable with it.

—*Do you consider yourself to be a social activist?*
I think that, up until recently, a good part of my time had been wrapped around raising a family and working, so I haven't taken on the role of a social activist. On the other hand, I have supported social activism; my husband is a social activist and I would call a lot

of my friends social activists. In my involvement with the Women's Centre I have also supported social activism—I support what the Women's Centre values.

—*Do you see yourself becoming more involved in social activism?*
Yes. I think as my family grows up I may get more opportunities. I'm going to Ottawa for the NAC convention and that is certainly an organization that is socially active. So I am participating, but there is a difference between participating and actually stepping into the role of social activist. I don't think I've done that. Partly because of my many obligations. I feel inspired by social activists; I see them doing more front line work than I have done. We'll see what the future brings.

—*What do you do at the Women's Centre?*
I am a co-chair of the board. First of all I volunteered to be on the board and then last year they needed someone to be the co-chair. Nobody else volunteered, so I got it by default.

Over the past year, I have chaired meetings, given input on decisions that the board has had to make, volunteered, and participated in fund-raising events. I also gave a presentation to the City of Calgary FCSS asking them for funding for the Centre.

—*Do you enjoy being co-chair?*
Yes. A good deal. I've enjoyed meeting different people at the Centre; it's a fun group to be with. And it is important for me to be involved in something.

—*What are your plans for the immediate future of the Women's Centre?*
I rely to a large extent on the evaluation that was done prior to my becoming a board member, and I trust in that to give us some direction over at least the next five years. It was a wonderful and

expansive report that fundamentally supported the role that the Women's Centre has been carrying on and the services we provide. It gave us principles to expand, but of course that's a matter of seeing what opportunity serves. To the extent that we can fundraise and get enough financial support, I see the maintenance and expansion of existing services.

—What do you think about the Women's Centre obtaining charitable status?
I think it's important for the longevity of the Centre because it gives us autonomy and credibility. For a lot of people who donate money to a cause, there's a sense that a certain screening process has taken place through the application for charitable status. Once you have that, people are probably more comfortable donating funds. We've been very fortunate over the first few years in having charitable status through Oxfam. But charitable status will give the Women's Centre control over our funding and responsibility for obtaining funding and providing receipts.

—What do you do for a living?
I am a civil engineer. Civil engineers are educated to work with municipal structures but I don't do any of that; I am mainly involved in economics.

I decided to become an engineer in my thirteenth year in high school in Ontario. When I was in school math and science were easy for me.

—What is it like to be a woman in a male-dominated field?
It is male-dominated, no question. I guess it's lonely. I think that you go through transitions in your life: from university into the early stages of your career, then the middle and latter stages. And there is an evolution of how you feel along the way. In university, you work so hard to be part of the group and you have a broad base of friends,

both male and female. When you get into the early stages of your career, you are working so much with men and trying to be part of the group. It's not until later that you realize that you can never really be part of the group. You start missing people, other women who you can communicate with, bond with, be with, relax with, but they are not there. It was later in my life that I started to seek out other women and that's partly why I came to the Women's Centre and supported them.

—As well as feeling lonely, do you also experience discrimination in the engineering field?
The simple answer is yes, but of course it's much more complex because there is discrimination everywhere in every aspect of society. It's very hard to identify discrimination that would provoke legal action. There's discrimination that would provoke response with a grievance at work and there's discrimination where you would say something directly to the individual or grit your teeth and bear it or ignore it. I always look to the solutions and the solutions are largely social. I have found that my peers are great people to work with. Once they get to know me and to work with me we make a great team. I don't think that they have discriminated against me, but that isn't to say that discrimination doesn't exist or that I haven't run across it. Perhaps it has happened and I didn't even see it. One of the easiest ways of surviving in a male field is not to see the discrimination. It is hard enough finding a life in the business field without taking on social battles at work which would make it doubly difficult.

—How is working and being a mother?
I couldn't have done it without a supportive husband. We have been fortunate in that I can go to work and he has been the primary caregiver for the past nine years. We have other support systems as well, but for me it is a constant battle between wanting to work,

enjoying the work, and yet wanting to spend time with the kids. It always involves balancing and trading. I guess when you think of it as work it gets harder, but when you think of it as your life it becomes easier.

—And the Women's Centre fits into that balance?
I joined a book club in 1990 and we meet once a month. That's how I found women friends. I came to the Women's Centre as well because I needed to connect with other women and I felt that I needed to give something back.

Glimpse into the Lives of Two Immigrant Women of Colour
Rosita Thorpe

I am somewhat uncomfortable being referred to as a "woman of colour." I consider all people of all racial categories as being born within a range of skin colours. No one is devoid of colour. Immigrants of colour have been (over the past 30 years) resettling in the Calgary community and contributing to the multiculturally diverse "changing face of Calgary." Included in this group are women of various shades of brown, who have joined immediate or extended family in seeking a better life in a new homeland. Women in this category face enormous challenges as they attempt to fit into their new social and cultural environment. They are more visible than other women in mainstream society, not only because of skin colour, but also because of the traditional lifestyles and customs of their cultures of origin. Many of these women face discrimination because of their limited ability to speak English.

This story contrasts the lives of two immigrant women of colour and explores the differences that separate them from one another. The first woman has a privileged lifestyle while the second woman experiences many obstacles to successful integration into a society that she perceives as exclusive rather than inclusive in its structural framework.

I arrived in this bustling metropolis, situated on the Bow River, nestled in the shadow of the majestic Rocky Mountains, in 1969, accompanying my husband, who had been recruited by the University of Calgary to be an assistant professor in the Department of Biological Sciences. We brought with us our infant son, who was three months old. As a young family with cultural roots in a Caribbean island, we wondered how we would adapt to the temperate climate of the prairies. But we were young and adventurous and, having lived in the USA for six years, were eager to resettle in another part of North America.

We had grown up learning about Canada in the British-based school system of Barbados. We knew that, like Barbados, Canada was a British Commonwealth country, with Queen Elizabeth II as Head of State, represented by a Governor General. I suppose, therefore, we already felt some kind of kinship with Canadians. We did not learn much about the Prairie provinces, but studied more about Central and Eastern Canada. We had never heard of Calgary until my husband saw a job position advertised by the University of Calgary and decided to research information about the city. He applied for the job and was hired.

Upon our arrival in Calgary, a professor representing the Department of Biological Sciences greeted us. He welcomed us to the university community and helped us immeasurably in settling into our new home. The neighbourhood where we lived for one year, before acquiring our permanent family home, was quiet with new apartments, well kept older homes, and a lovely park across the street. I observed that there were no persons of colour occupying our apartment building or the homes in this area. I eagerly looked for persons with whom I could identify racially as I visited the park every day with my infant son. They never appeared at any time during the year we lived there. I began to wonder whether Calgary did indeed have any persons of colour.

We knew of one Barbadian family living in Calgary. We called this family upon our arrival and they welcomed and entertained us on many occasions. They became very dear friends of our family and have remained so for over 30 years. The husband was employed in the oil and gas industry. Through this family we met several other black professional families. Even within this intimate social group, we met more Caucasians than persons of colour. We did, however, attend many Caribbean events where we saw immigrants of colour. At these functions we would often comment that we had never before seen so many black people in Calgary. During the late '60s and early '70s in the Calgary area, it seemed as though persons of colour were not an integral component of the community.

My husband's colleagues at the University warmly welcomed us, and soon our social contacts centred on this select group. At professional as well as personal social events, we were usually the only persons of colour.

When our children were very young, I would take them shopping with me at the local supermarket. Shoppers in the line with me would ask if they could touch the soft, natural curls on my children's heads. They would also compliment me on my naturally curly hair and tell me that Caucasians paid a lot of money for the same look through a salon-produced perm. I would thank them graciously for their compliments and assure them that when the weather was hot and humid (as it is in Barbados), I longed to have smoother, less curly hair. We would concur that human beings are never happy with what they have been blessed with and always seem to long for what others have. What a pity!

As a family we encountered a minimal number of blatant racially motivated experiences. I will share with you the few we have experienced. When my daughter, who was born in Calgary, was three years old, I enrolled her in a preschool program held in the basement of an Anglican Church. One day, a young boy who was also three years old said to her, "Tell your mother to wash your hands, because they are dirty and then they will be clean and white like mine." My daughter replied, "My hands are not dirty; my hands are brown." When I went to pick her up at the school, she was crying. She continued to attend the preschool and soon forgot this unfortunate incident. It didn't seem to emotionally affect her. I decided, however, to talk to our children about their racial heritage and explain why their skin was brown and why their hair was curly. I told them that the world is made up of people of many colours and hair textures. I told them that no one person is better than another, although we are all different. I knew that I was responsible to ensure that my children, at this young age, began to develop a healthy perception of their value to society. My role was to assist them in building increasing levels of self-esteem and self-confidence.

During her young adult years, my daughter was challenged to test her self-confidence when she came face to face with a blatant incident of racial discrimination. She and her friends decided to visit a local nightclub in downtown Calgary. Three of them were women of colour and the other young woman was white. When they approached the entrance of the club, the man at the door invited the young white woman to enter, but denied entry to the three women of colour. He said that the club's policy was not to accept persons of colour, since they usually "cause trouble." My daughter responded that he was stereotyping, which is against the human rights laws of Canada and Alberta and which could cause trouble for his business. She also told him that he did not know her and could not assume that because she was a black person she would cause trouble. He persisted in denying the three women of colour entry into the club. All the women left and the white girl, furious with this man's unacceptable behavior, called her father, who was in senior management with a local TV station. The young women of colour were interviewed on the evening news. The *Calgary Herald* picked up the story and the exposure was tremendous.

The overall effect was that my daughter and the other women of colour received numerous calls from other students of colour attending SAIT and Mount Royal College, who had also been discriminated against by this particular nightclub. My daughter documented all the incidents and filed a complaint with the Alberta Human Rights Commission. The nightclub owners were ordered to write an apology to the victims of their discriminatory business practices. My daughter is now almost 30 years old and a professional in the USA. Recently, while discussing this past incident, she told me that she feels that the Human Rights Commission should have warned the nightclub about future legal action if they continued such unacceptable business practices. She was disappointed with the inconsequential action of the HRC. She is convinced that this particular nightclub continued to discriminate against persons of colour.

As a result, our family became more aware of racism in Calgary and in Canada. But we did not allow this encounter with discrimination to consume our daily lives or to make us wary of all white Canadians. We respect and value people as individuals and judge them by their individual behavior, rather than by the colour of their skin. We expect others to respond to us likewise. I believe that this incident changed our young adult son's and daughter's perceptions of the integration of black persons in Calgary and Canada. Our daughter, in particular, began to feel that she would never feel at home in Calgary, where persons of colour were not in prominent positions of authority. After she graduated from the University of Calgary in 1994, she left to work and live in many parts of the world. Both our son and daughter now work as professionals in the USA and are very content with their choice to relocate to a community where they feel accepted. Atlanta, Georgia, among many other large American cities, has the largest number of successful, young, black professionals.

I became more aware of the attitudes of Calgarians to diversity in our community when I went to work, in 1983, for a local agency whose clientele primarily consists of immigrants and refugees. My work involved multiculturalism and diversity training for mainstream Canadians within diverse organizations, including government, education and healthcare organizations, as well as non-profit and community service agencies. I facilitated skills development training for many Calgarians: professionals, students, and immigrants and refugees resettling in the community. Training focused on valuing diversity in the community. Learning strategies encouraged the collaboration of diverse individuals and groups toward facilitating the successful integration of immigrants and refugees in the community. Immigrants need and want to participate in and contribute to their new community. In return they want to be recognized as valued citizens. Calgary needs to adopt practices and policies that reflect the increasing diversity of our multicultural population.

In my work within the agency as well as in the community, I interacted with immigrants and refugees on a daily basis. During my 16 years with this agency, my eyes were opened to the enormous challenges that other immigrant families experience during the resettlement process.

The following story highlights a common experience of many marginalized immigrants in Canada whose skin colour is not white and whose first language is not English. In the case of this particular family, both the husband and wife were professionals in their country of origin and were accepted as immigrants to Canada because they had doctorate degrees and because they were highly competent in the English language. Yet they were consistently denied employment in their specific career fields as well as in other professional fields.

The husband had been invited by a University of Calgary professor, whom he had met at a scientific conference in India, to collaborate on a research project. That was the family's sole reason for immigrating to Calgary. Throughout his entire time in this position, the husband was never permanently employed. He was always employed temporarily, through small scientific grants with low pay and with no hope of securing a permanent job. When the professor left the University for a better job, this highly qualified immigrant man was suddenly jobless and depressed about this crisis in his life. He felt that Canada had filled his life with false hope, since Canada Immigration valued his qualifications, but not his right to be professionally employed. He was continually praised at the University for his skills and knowledge. But he felt that this praise was not honest, since no one would hire him for a permanent job. The family felt that their decision to immigrate to Canada might have been an unwise one. They had enjoyed a high standard of living in India, since they had both worked as professionals. They had also had an important status in their community, where they were highly respected.

They swallowed their pride and decided that since they had made the decision to relocate here, they would strive to successfully integrate. They wanted their young son to have a good future in Canada, and for this reason they would persevere. The husband decided to apply for a job as a salesman, so that he could support his family. He had no previous experience in this area and did not understand the philosophy of selling or care for the challenges it presented. He decided, however, that any job was better than no job. It was a very difficult decision for the family, since work in India defines a person's status in the community. A professional never assumes a job role that is not in his field. He was a scientist, a chemist, and he should be employed in a job that reflected his professional qualifications.

His wife was emotionally distressed over this turn of events, because she witnessed daily how this situation challenged her husband's self-esteem and self-worth. She would meet me for coffee to discuss her family's situation. She would often comment on how lucky our family was and would blame her family's bad luck on their inability to be as fluent in English as my husband and I were. She also considered her image as a quiet, shy, Indian woman, as compared with my outgoing personality, to be a stumbling block to her acceptance by Canadians. She decided that she should practice being more self-assertive. She explained to me that, as a South Asian woman accustomed to valuing the ideals of her culture, she was emotionally devastated by the hurtful criticism she daily encountered because she chose to practice her cultural traditions. She wore her traditional costume of the graceful and colourful sari with pride. Soon her pride was shattered when young Calgarians laughed at her and taunted her about her style of dress. They suggested to her in most unacceptable language and tone of voice that she should go back to her own country. On one occasion, when she was walking to Prince's Island Park to celebrate Canada Day, some teenagers threw stones at her and uttered abusive taunts. She was humiliated by this societal rejection and wondered why they had chosen to relocate to Canada.

Before deciding to immigrate, the family often told others how confident they felt about relocating to Canada. Their decision was based on the favourable accounts they had read, or heard from friends, about the liberal attitudes of Canadians to the acceptance of differences in others. They had read about the multiculturalism policies of Canada, which supported the retention of immigrant cultural traditions and values. After they came to Canada, they wondered why Canada had developed policies that did not seem to work for those whom they welcomed to this land. They often said that the multiculturalism policy was more words than action.

The wife decided that she would have to work in order to assist her husband in paying the bills. She would see a job advertised in the newspaper and would call to find out about it. She would be told very quickly that the job had been filled. Then she would continue to see the same job advertised in the newspaper. This happened often. She decided to find out whether she was being discriminated against based on her accent. She asked a Canadian friend to call about the same job. The Canadian woman not only found out that the position was still open, but she was also invited to submit her resume. I am sure that you can well imagine the South Asian woman's anger when she discovered that indeed she been rebuffed because of her East-

Indian-accented English.

When she was finally granted a job interview, she was told that she would have to change her style of dress and cut her long braid if she ever hoped to be employed in a Canadian workplace. She decided to follow these instructions even though it was a very painful decision to cut her long, beautiful hair. She would comment on the unfairness of a society that makes certain people go through a total transformation to fit into a prescribed societal mold. She felt as if she was losing her soul to gain the acceptance of mainstream Canadians.

She was also instructed to remove the red dot on her forehead, which in her culture identified her as a married woman. This was traumatic for her and for her husband, because if an East Indian married woman removes the red dot from her forehead, it signifies to the world that she is a widow. Her husband was very upset with this advice from a mainstream Canadian. As they would often share with others, nothing positive came of these dramatic changes that they made to fit into their new society. They still felt rejected and disapproved of.

The family experienced a worse emotional state when insensitive teenage classmates began to perpetrate cruel racist acts against the teenage son. The teenagers teased the son about his skin colour, his clothes, which were not name brands, his accented English, and his vegetarian lunch. They teased him because he was not allowed, at 13 years of age, to attend junior high school dances. In East Indian culture, young men and women are not allowed to attend co-educational socials, especially when couple dancing is allowed. Intimate physical contact between males and females is not acceptable. The young teenager was not comfortable with these school socials and shared his preference with his classmates, who then decided to label him. He was very frustrated and disappointed with their cruel response and decided to stick to friends who were East Indian like himself. He became more interested in the activities of the family's ethnocultural group and seemed to finally find a niche for himself.

The family decided to relocate to the USA, where the father finally secured a professional job with a scientific laboratory. His qualifications were highly valued and financially rewarded. The family had at last found a place where life seemed to be smiling down on them. The young man is now a university student and is performing very well academically and looking forward to a financially rewarding career in the future. They have regained a socio-economic status of which they are proud, and their pride in their achievements as East Indian immigrants is fully restored. It is unfortunate that this benefit was not bestowed on this family in Canada, which was, and probably still is, their country of choice.

Over the years, I have met many other immigrant families of colour who have had similar experiences. On the other hand, I also know many immigrant families of colour who have never had to give up their original status to succeed in Canada. Some of these families would argue that immigrating to Canada and making changes in their original lifestyles and customs resulted in enormous success. I can never seem to find plausible reasons why some individuals experience traumatic cross-cultural hurdles in their new lives, while others seem to surmount the obstacles.

THANK YOU WOMEN'S CENTRE
Anonymous

I am Mexican and I have a Bachelor's Degree in Agronomy. I moved to Calgary in May 1996 to complete my PhD at the University of Calgary in the Department of Biological Sciences, with a full 36-month scholarship from the Mexican government. When I arrived, I had only the clothes that I wore in my home city, which of course were not appropriate for the different weather in Calgary. With help from my professor at the University of Calgary, and from a Latin couple I met in Calgary, I was able to set up a lovely, simple home with beautiful plants.

I completed my courses and prerequisites at the U of C while raising my beautiful boy, named Luis Jorge, who is now four years old. I did this with the valuable help of my 26-year-old niece, Claudia, whom Luis Jorge loves like a mother. Claudia is a very soft, charming, young girl. She learned English by watching cartoons on TV with my little one. Claudia has helped him retain his Spanish and English as well as his Mexican heritage and Canadian culture.

It took some time for the three of us to settle in Calgary and to adjust to a new lifestyle, new weather, and a new language too. We speak Spanish at home, eat mainly Mexican food, including hot peppers, and listen to Spanish music.

After the 36 months of the scholarship, my advisor and I sent in an application to the Mexican government for extended funding to continue the program. We had known since the beginning that 36 months was not enough time to finish the degree. In 1999, after I did not receive my monthly allowance, we contacted the Mexican government and found out that they had never received the application for extended funding. We sent in another application immediately, but had to wait two months for processing. In the meantime, I received no money from the scholarship that January or February, and had no income at all. We had no money for rent, food, or tuition fees.

At the University, I was lucky enough to run into one of the staff of the Women's Centre, whom I had met before under different circumstances. She said, "Come to the Centre, and we'll see how we can help." This is how I came to the Women's Centre and got to know the kind staff and volunteers. They have bought groceries for us on more than one occasion, connected me to another organization where we could get much-needed clothing, invited us to participate in the collective kitchen, and provided emotional support and encouragement. I have kept in touch with the Centre since then. I am very grateful for all the help I've received and hope that the Centre will continue to support women to keep moving forward, succeed, be productive, and accomplish their goals.

The volunteers and staff at the Women's Centre are always helpful and friendly. At the collective kitchen, I have found friends and mothers who have taught me new recipes and have helped me become a better mother, student, and person. In the future, I hope to contribute to the community as a professional woman. Thank you, Women's Centre, for being there.

A FAMILY MATTER
Anonymous

My sister recently attempted suicide. The shock waves have gone through her family, my family, and our family, and have rippled into the families of in-laws, the lives of friends, and the thoughts of her neighbours. We are all gawkers at the scene of a terrible crash. Friends wonder aloud *how* she did it with the same curiosity as they wonder *why*. Some empathize with the depression that drove her to this extreme. Some feel guilty. They say they "should have known," or "should have done something" as though some magical task might have prevented my sister from trying to kill herself. Others are bewildered. They think she has a good life, but they see it only from the outside. They shrug their shoulders and move on. I am having trouble moving on. I am her sister. We shared the same home, parents, and lives. I see her life from the inside and it is right next to mine.

Ever since my sister decided to announce her unhappiness, I picture our family in a new frame—a frame that includes the kind of pain that leads to suicide. Our childhood has suddenly become crowded with unresolved issues. As children, we were never friends. Our disagreements were typical sibling rivalry, but I always knew there was more to it than that. We were so different. I felt she despised me. I was an embarrassment—so uncool. She was the pretty one. She tortured me about my frumpiness, my bad hair, and my bookish interests. She was volatile, screaming at my mother on her way out the door about how she would wear what she wanted and see whom she pleased. I watched my mother cry as the door slammed and I picked up the pieces. I felt sorry for my mother.

My father was absent for most of the scenes, already at work. And at night, he seemed not to notice after a few drinks. He was emotionally absent, even when he was physically present. Nevertheless, my parents were good enough, I thought. My family was within the range of normal, I thought. Now, looking at that family picture in its new frame, even this minimally acceptable assessment is in jeopardy. Maybe our family isn't good enough after all.

I did well in school, handled my troubles myself, always had a job, and paid my way through university. But my family did not celebrate my success and happiness with much enthusiasm, at least not in the brass-band-and-ticker-tape-parade way that I imagined. We did not make a big deal about me for fear that it might make my sister feel bad. I told myself I understood, but I never did.

I suddenly remember petty resentments, and I am shocked by what has been lurking so long in my subconscious. My sister had new dresses for big occasions. I remember the ill-fitting hand-me-downs I wore at my graduation. I remember wondering why that was all I deserved. She had an elaborate wedding. At about the same time her marriage was failing, I had a few friends over after my own small wedding. I learned to narrow the scope of my joy in order to narrow the scope of my sister's pain.

I know that she has not been happy during our adult lives. She always cared too much about what other people thought. She defined herself only through the reactions of others. She had to have the right clothes, the right hairstyle, the right friends. She had a lovely house, filled with lovely things all prettily displayed. She entertained well—she always had something delicious to eat and wine in the fridge. There were problems, always discussed over drinks. No one questioned her role in her problems. She married a terrible man. The general consensus was that she was blameless for the failure of her marriage.

I helped her out however I could. My life was going well and I was able to help. I did not realize that I was enabling. I did not see her emerging alcoholism. Or was I in denial? I sometimes wondered why my efforts on her behalf consistently failed to change her circumstances. I felt like I was jumping through hoops, pushing the boulder up the mountain with Sisyphus. But I forced that feeling away and continued my efforts. I was still trying to have a model family and to stay connected; there is no connection like a family connection. I now know my sister is more connected to my family through alcoholism than through me. That leaves me quite orphaned.

I am still close enough to the revelation of her alcoholism and my own sudden re-analysis of my family to see her suicide attempt as the ultimate selfish act in a life of selfishness. I am angry. We must all once again drop everything and pay attention to her. It brings me back to my uncomfortable childhood, when I did not like her very much but learned to dwell on her problems and deny my own joy. Now I am angry at a grown woman's inability to fix her life and at her disregard for those she would have left behind, including me. I know alcoholism is a disease. But an awful part of me feels that she made the choices that resulted in this disaster. She does have a role in her problems. I am tired of seeing her portrayed as the victim of circumstance. She is an adult now, the adult child of an alcoholic, just like me, and she should know better.

I am grieving the loss of my sister. I can no longer pretend our relationship was good, and I can no longer pretend my family was good enough. I cannot count on her to be my family or to love me. She cannot even love herself.

We came from a home in which words like "divorce" and "alcoholism" were whispered over our heads among the adults. She learned to keep up appearances well. So did I. I never approached her directly about her problems because naming them honestly wasn't what we had learned to do. I only tried to help her step over them. Did I get a perverse satisfaction from her need? I look back on the help I gave her and I realize that it was useless. I now recognize my complicity. I cared for her physical circumstances; I failed at caring for her soul. I wish that I could give her happiness like a new coat to wear, but I cannot. She has to find it for herself, and so far, she has chosen not to. I have to respect that choice. The time has come for me to let her go. This realization has come late and at a desperate time. Like my sister, I also worry about what others will think, and how my lack of action might be misinterpreted as a lack of love. I cannot do anything for her. I will honestly believe that she is capable of helping herself. It is her life, for her to live as she chooses. No one can shape it for her, not even me.

And what else will I do? I will celebrate my happiness, finally, after all these years. I am still happily married—I have a family I love and a home in which I am at peace. I have a dynamic group of friends that I think of as my chosen family. I will cherish these relationships. I will take care of myself. I have energy and love to spare. Happiness is hard work, but worth it. Misery is hard work too, but not worth the effort. Maybe if I had celebrated my happiness all along, my sister would have seen happiness as a desirable goal. I have learned that I want to feel the full force of joy, even though I must also feel the full force of pain.

I believe that we are all part of something bigger than ourselves. For the sake of simplicity, I can call it God. I know that there are forces beyond my control and understanding that keep the universe moving and hold me lovingly within its vast embrace. I welcome them with an open heart. All I can do for my sister now is hope that she will feel this embrace as those same forces reach out to her. I am a part of that embrace and I love her.

JOURNEY TO WOMYNHOOD
Paz Pino

What initially brought me to the Women's Center was my need to help wimmin. Yet what continually brings me back is the wimmin who have helped me. In the few months that I've been at the Women's Centre, I have found a balance in my own journey toward womynhood and toward the personal and political in my life. I am a radical lesbian feminist.

Radical feminism has given me the tools to stop living on the surface and to go to the root in my life. My whole being has fallen deeper inside radical feminism and it has given me a new awareness and a fuller understanding of myself and of the connection that I have with those around me.

When I look at society around us, I notice that a lot of us live unaware of our surroundings. Yet the steps we unconsciously (or consciously) take to fulfill our short term needs affect the less fortunate around us. These steps can often prevent the less fortunate from having access to the tools they need to empower themselves. We choose to ignore that our empowerment and their lack of empowerment are interconnected—that one often affects the other. I want to learn to break this vicious cycle and fully understand how we got to where we are before I take the steps toward where I want to go.

Radical feminism means fighting all oppressions (sexism, racism, able-ism, homophobia, and so forth) all the time. As a lesbian, I recognize that I have a different viewpoint from heterosexual wimmin, and as a Latina, I have a different viewpoint from white wimmin. (And as a light skinned Latina, I recognize the different viewpoint I have from my visibly recognizable sisters of color.) As a radical feminist, I attempt to follow certain beliefs or slogans in my life. The first one is "the personal is political," which means, to me, that I should apply what I believe on a political level to my personal life. For example, since I agree that saving the environment makes good political sense, I need to take responsibility by recycling. The second slogan is "the means are the end," which means that the steps I take in the present will lead me to what I want to achieve in the future. In other words, instead of just talking about changing the world and doing nothing, I start making the changes in myself which enable me to change the environment around me.

In the not-so-long-ago past, I was a hard, defiant, and intimidating person. I was so strong-minded in my beliefs that I never allowed any space for healthy opposition. Often when wimmin heard that I was radical, they simply saw the extremity before they saw the person and instantly their judgments and defenses came up. I ended up playing the role they wanted to see. Everything was cut and dry for me, and those who crossed the wrong path with me were instantly cut out of my life. I was so determined in my passion to fight for wimmin's rights and lesbian rights that my defiance was scaring wimmin away.

It really hit me when someone recently told me she saw me as "dangerous." This made me take a step back and evaluate what my priorities in life were, who I was, and what I was projecting about myself to the wimmin around me. It broke my heart to realize that it was my own doing that had led some amazing, beautiful, kind wimmin to part ways with me. I hadn't given any space for growth and movement in my life and it finally hit me that my work, my feminist stance, was burning me out. I hadn't given space to simply agree to disagree.

I realized that I was still thinking from my head instead of living from my heart. I was still analyzing everything without feeling what it meant to me. I had come to the realization that I had not yet fallen to my root and that this defense, this barrier I was putting up against patriarchy (and, ironically, against wimmin), was burning me out. I was spending so much time fighting that I had stopped listening to wimmin, and thus my work had become futile.

When I'm at the Women's Centre, I meet amazing wimmin who take my breath away. These wimmin, their voices, their language moves me. It carries me. And it is bliss. They remind me how precious moments are and how each journey is a journey to womynhood.

I think…no rather, I feel that when I first came to the Women's Centre I treated it like a job, where I gave my blood each Friday, pulled down my sleeve, and then went home. Now I feel like the Centre is my saving grace where wimmin laugh with me, sing with me, and cry with me. The Women's Centre has become a place where we share our lives with each other. No matter how hard life is outside, inside this space we each become significant, we each become special.

WOMAN TIME
Ashlyn D'Aoust

I have been volunteering at the Women's Centre since the autumn of 1998. During that time, I have learned a great deal about women's issues and about the plight of disadvantaged women in Calgary. I am in an odd position: I have never had to go without food or shelter, but I am attending university on student loans and living hand to mouth. My perspective includes the worlds of both advantaged and disadvantaged women. In my experience, the Women's Centre offers women a place that respects them simply as women, regardless of social or economic standing. Once in the door, all women are equal.

All women who enter are not the same, of course. The variety of personalities adds to the Centre's atmosphere. Volunteers and clients create a lively mix: wealthy, comfortable, and poor; African, North or South American, Asian, and European; pro-choice and anti-abortion; naturalists and environmentalists; fur-wearers and anti-fur activists; religious observers and atheists; heterosexuals and homosexuals; and so on. The Centre offers an open and encouraging place where different views are discussed, debated, and welcomed.

Patience is a virtue, they say. I am learning the value of this attribute. I always run on a schedule, timed almost to the last minute, and the schedule of the Women's Centre baffled me at first. There is no rushing; clients are welcome in whenever they choose to arrive and are not hurried out because the workday is over or because the phone is ringing. Everyone gets the attention due to her, in due time. Instead of running on rat-race-treadmill time, the Women's Centre runs on "woman time." Whatever length of time each woman needs, each woman gets. I have to adjust to this system each time I return to the Centre, and I always dislike having to re-adjust when I leave; I prefer the steady, slower, patient, woman-friendly pace.

Often when I visit the Women's Centre, I witness amazing feats due to the ingenuity and the dedication of staff and volunteers. Individuals take on extra responsibility or go the extra mile when clients are in need. Food and gift hampers are collected and delivered right to the door. Teams of people are co-ordinated to assist needy clients with tasks. Women who lose their direction are put to work as volunteers to give them perspective and camaraderie. Women with poor social skills are integrated and valued.

Being at the Women's Centre has challenged me to develop my tolerance level. While all women are welcome and accepted, not all women get along. No one likes, or is liked by, everyone. Being part of the Women's Centre not only means being accepted and valued as a person, it also means extending that courtesy to all others who enter. I have explored and expanded this area of myself and hope to continue to do so.

The long arms of the Women's Centre are quite impressive. The troops assemble to support important issues or to lobby for funds to keep the Centre open. Most do not show up on the front lines ready for open battle; most work as part of the infrastructure. If the infrastructure does not hold, the whole system comes crashing down. When the city threatened to remove funding, a large-scale phone/fax/e-mail campaign was undertaken and the funders reconsidered. A small but steadfast group attended the proceedings in quiet support, myself included. The extended women's community of Calgary came together to offer support and to assist us.

The Women's Centre has given me some needed perspective. I have come to consider issues with their effects on women in mind, not simply their effects on me personally. The Women's Centre offers me an island of femininity in a male-oriented world. This space offers women sanctuary from a world where male voices and opinions dominate. In this space we not only have the freedom to voice our own opinions and concerns, we are also able to hear the opinions and concerns of other women—women whose voices may be drowned out outside the Centre. Being able to hear other women's voices is as important as being able to voice my own thoughts. The Women's Centre is the only place I have ever been where women are always heard and never dismissed. In my opinion, this is the greatest triumph of the Women's Centre.

FROM MARGIN TO CENTRE[1]: ORGANIZING FOR WOMEN'S RIGHTS
Julie Black

This year, over 4000 social justice groups from 153 countries are participating in The World March of Women to **end poverty** and to **end violence against women**.

The World March of Women is a march against women's poverty in a world of wealth. It is a march against violence against women when- and wherever it happens, whether in times of war or in times of peace. It is a march against the violence and the systemic discrimination faced by lesbians throughout the world. It is a march of sisterhood in diversity, an expression of women's determination to build different lives for all the women of the world.

Sickened by the triumph of greed and exploitation over human rights and social justice, women's rights activists call for rallies, workshops, and symbolic actions to raise voices and hearts in protest. What can such a call to action mean for Calgary women? If you look at the official views of our city, it shouldn't mean much. After all, as the City of Calgary letterhead proclaims, this is *Calgary: The Best Place to Live!* In reality, many women, and certainly anyone who has been involved at the community level with women in this city, would know that the World March of Women is about Canada, Alberta, and Calgary as much as about any other part of the world.

SOME STATISTICS ON POVERTY AND WEALTH:

In 1999 Calgary boasted an unemployment rate of 5.5%, less than the national average of 7.6%. Per capita income was 23% above the national average. Calgary exports were worth an estimated $22 billion.[2] But, as a study of 1995 incomes confirms, 20% of Calgarians fit the definition of living in poverty, exactly the same as the Canadian average.[3] How can this be?

SOCIAL ASSISTANCE:

- *All welfare rates in Canada fall far below the poverty line, ranging from 20% – 76% below.[4]*
- *In Alberta, a single parent with two children is eligible for only $939 a month from social assistance. The National Child Benefit adds only another $114 a month.[5]*

MINIMUM WAGE:

- *In Alberta, "being employed helps in reducing poverty but is not necessarily a guard against it." 77% of the 106,610 poor families in Alberta were employed for at least a part of 1995. 44% worked full-time, at minimum wage or just above it.[6]*
- *Despite the recent raise of the Alberta minimum wage to $5.90/hour and the abolishment of the discriminatory student rate, Alberta low-income earners have been steadily losing ground to increases in the cost of living. For example, the 1977 minimum wage of $3/hour translates into $8/hour in 1998 terms.[7] This has a profound effect on women, since women comprise two-thirds of Canada's minimum wage earners.[8]*

INEQUITABLE WAGES:

- *Canada has the fifth largest wage gap between men and women out of the world's 29 most developed countries.[9]*
- *Women in Canada earn 73% of what men earn for full-time, full-year work.*
- *For women with disabilities, even in their prime earning years (ages 35 – 53), the ratio lowers to 55%.[10]*
- *Other studies show that the average income of Aboriginal women is*

$11,900 compared to $17,500 for Aboriginal men and $17,600 for all women in Canada.[11]

- *Even when matched for age and level of education, post-1976 immigrant women have lower incomes than average.*[12]

SOME STATISTICS ON VIOLENCE AGAINST WOMEN:

Violence against women and children is a widespread problem in this city.

- *According to the provincial government, there are 19 women's shelters in Alberta, two second-stage housing facilities, and eight rural family violence prevention centres.*

- *In 1998/99, 4,923 women and 6,002 children were admitted to shelter. However, 3,415 women and children were referred to Alberta Family and Social Services for alternate housing.*[13] *This is a polite way to say that there aren't enough shelters in all areas and that usually shelters are full.*

- *Calgary Police Services receives over 1,000 calls per month about "domestic violence."*[14] *And we know that most women experiencing violence don't call the police.*

- *Canada is second only to the United States in imprisoning our population. In 1998, we put 143 people per 100,000 in jail.*[15] *Aboriginal, Inuit, and Métis women and men are vastly over-represented in these jails. This high rate is typical of colonized countries.*[16]

A CALL TO ACTION: CHANGING THESE STATISTICS

The World March of Women is an opportunity to challenge these and other inequities and injustices.

The World March of Women was officially launched on International Women's Day, March 8, 2000, in Canada, Peru, Brazil, Bolivia, Denmark, Romania, Nepal, Pakistan, Morocco, Zambia, and in many other countries. The Hong Kong launch supported the "Purple

Rose" campaign against sex trafficking. In the Democratic Republic of Congo, activists held a "day without women," where women stayed at home to mourn their sisters, brothers, husbands, and children who were killed during the conflicts. In Croatia, women held a press conference called "Appeal against Poverty." In Calgary, local women's groups held several launches aimed at raising awareness of the March and inviting women to join the campaign.

The World March of Women wraps up in October 2000, in time for the International Day for the Elimination of Poverty. Events will be held throughout the world, including Parliament Hill, Ottawa, and outside The International Monetary Fund, Washington D.C on October 15, and outside the United Nations, New York City on October 17. The Women's Centre of Calgary will hold a poverty workshop to mark the end of the event.

The end of the World March of Women isn't the end of the efforts to bring together the women of the world. The hope is that women's global connections will continue and grow. This new era of women's rights activism faces severe and troubling challenges. But never before have women been so linked with one another, so able to learn from each other and to build common cause and co-ordinated action.

There has never been a better time to get involved. Join the March, join the Women's Centre, or find another way to support the human rights of women.

For more information on the World March of Women, contact the Women's Centre or visit www.ffq.qc.ca.

ENDNOTES

1. Title borrowed from bell hooks, *Feminist Theory from Margin to Centre* (1984).

2. City of Calgary, "Annual Report 1999", www.gov.calgary.ab.ca

3. Inter City Forum on Social Policy, *No Safeguards: A Profile of Urban Poverty in Alberta,* (Edmonton: February 2000).

4. National Council of Welfare, "Welfare Incomes 1992", (Ottawa, 1993).

5. Alberta Human Resources and Employment, "Welfare's Financial Benefits Summary", (August 1, 1999).

6. Inter City Forum on Social Policy, ibid, vi.

7. Selby, Jim, "Tear Out Guide", *Labour News*, (Edmonton: March 1998).

8. Statistics Canada, "Snapshot Report for January, February and March", (Ottawa: 1998).

9. Organization for Economic Co-operation and Development, "OECD in Figures", (Paris: OECD, 1999).

10. Statistics Canada, 1993.

11. Royal Commission on Aboriginal Peoples, ibid.

12. Marie Drolet and Rene Morisette, "To What Extent are Canadians Exposed to Low Income?" (Ottawa: Statistics Canada Income Division, 1999).

13. Government of Alberta, 1998/99 statistics, www.gov.ab.ca

14. Private conversation, January 2000.

15. Canadian Association of Elizabeth Fry Associations, 2000.

16. Greer, 1994. Quoted in *Black Eyes All of the Time: Intimate Violence, Aboriginal Women and the Justice System,* 21.